REBUILDING FINANCIAL STABILITY

A Practical Guide to Debt-Free Living and Future Planning

Robert Knight

To my mum and dad,

Whose unwavering support and guidance have shaped my journey,

To the love of my life,

Whose presence fills my days with joy and meaning,

And to my three wonderful kids,

Who inspire me every day with their boundless energy and love.

"Do not save what is left after spending, but spend what is left after saving."

— WARREN BUFFETT

PREFACE

The journey to financial stability is not just about numbers and budgets; it's about reclaiming control over your life and future. In a world where economic uncertainties have become the norm, achieving financial stability has never been more crucial. Whether you are overwhelmed by debt, striving to improve your credit score, or planning for a secure future, this book is your comprehensive guide to navigating the financial landscape with confidence and clarity.

Throughout my career, I have witnessed the transformative power of financial literacy and disciplined planning. The ability to manage money wisely is not an innate skill but a learned one. It requires knowledge, tools, and the right mindset. This book aims to provide you with all three, offering practical advice, actionable strategies, and insightful exercises to help you achieve financial independence and build a secure future.

The recent global challenges have underscored the importance of being prepared for the unexpected. Financial stability is not merely about accumulating wealth but about creating a resilient foundation that can weather any storm. It is about making informed decisions, setting realistic goals, and cultivating habits that lead to lasting financial health.

This book is structured to guide you step-by-step through the essential aspects of financial planning. From understanding your current financial situation to advanced investment strategies and retirement planning, each chapter is designed to equip you with the knowledge and confidence needed to take control of your financial destiny.

As you embark on this journey, remember that financial stability is a continuous process, not a one-time achievement. It requires regular reviews, adjustments, and a commitment to learning. But with dedication and the right strategies, you can achieve a life of financial freedom and security.

I hope this book serves as a valuable resource, empowering you to make informed decisions and take proactive steps toward a brighter financial future. Here's to building a life of stability, independence, and endless possibilities.

TABLE OF CONTENTS

INTRODUCTION

Welcome to "Rebuilding Financial Stability: A Practical Guide to Debt-Free Living and Future Planning." This book is designed to provide you with comprehensive knowledge, practical tools, and actionable strategies to achieve financial independence and build a secure future. Whether you are struggling with debt, aiming to improve your credit, or planning for early retirement, this guide will help you navigate your financial journey with confidence and clarity.

The Importance Of Financial Stability

In today's fast-paced and unpredictable world, financial stability is more critical than ever. The recent changes post-COVID have posed daunting challenges, prompting many to reassess their financial priorities and strategies. Achieving financial stability is not just about managing money; it's about creating a foundation that allows you to weather economic uncertainties, support your family, and pursue your goals without the constant stress of financial insecurity.

Understanding The Journey

This book takes you on a comprehensive journey through the essential aspects of financial planning:

1. **Building a Strong Financial Foundation**: Understand your current financial situation, set realistic goals, and create a budget to manage your finances effectively.
2. **Managing Debt and Improving Credit**: Learn practical

steps for managing debt, improving your credit score, and freeing yourself from financial burdens.

3. **Saving and Investing**: Explore strategies for saving money, investing wisely, and building wealth over time.

4. **Risk Management and Estate Planning**: Discover how to protect your assets, plan, and ensure your loved ones are taken care of.

5. **Achieving Financial Independence and Early Retirement (FIRE)**: Embrace the principles of the FIRE movement to save aggressively, spend mindfully, and invest strategically to achieve financial independence and retire early.

6. **Sustaining Financial Independence**: Learn advanced strategies for maintaining financial independence, managing your wealth, and adapting to life changes.

Psychological And Emotional Aspects

Financial challenges often bring significant psychological and emotional stress. This book acknowledges these aspects and provides guidance on how to manage stress, stay motivated, and maintain a positive mindset throughout your financial journey. By addressing these psychological factors, we aim to empower you to implement the strategies discussed effectively and with greater resilience.

Building Financial Literacy

Financial literacy is the cornerstone of financial stability. Throughout this book, we emphasize the importance of continuous learning and staying informed about financial trends, strategies, and best practices. By enhancing your financial literacy, you can make informed decisions, adapt to changes, and navigate financial challenges with confidence.

Practical Tools And Workbook Activities

To help you apply the concepts discussed, this book includes practical tools, worksheets, and workbook activities. These resources are designed to guide you in setting goals, tracking progress, and adjusting your financial plan. By engaging with these activities, you can create a personalized financial strategy that aligns with your unique goals and circumstances.

Preparing For Life's Transitions

Life is full of major events and transitions that can significantly affect your financial situation. This book provides strategies for navigating these key life events, such as career changes, marriage, parenthood, and retirement. By understanding and planning for these transitions, you can make informed decisions and maintain financial stability throughout life's various stages.

Finding Purpose And Fulfillment In Financial Independence

Financial independence is not just about money; it is about having the freedom to live life on your own terms. As you achieve financial independence, it is important to find purpose and fulfillment beyond financial goals. Pursue your passions, engage in meaningful activities, and build a life that brings you joy and satisfaction.

Encouraging A Holistic Approach To Financial Planning

A holistic approach to financial planning considers all aspects of your life, including your personal values, goals, and relationships. This book encourages you to integrate your financial plan with your overall life plan, ensuring that your financial decisions align with your broader aspirations and well-being.

Inspiring Future Generations

By embracing the principles and strategies outlined in this book, you can inspire future generations to achieve financial independence and stability. Share your knowledge and experiences with family and friends, and encourage them to take control of their financial futures. Together, we can build a financially literate and empowered society.

Final Thoughts

"Rebuilding Financial Stability: A Practical Guide to Debt-Free

Living and Future Planning" equips you with the knowledge and tools to achieve financial independence and build a secure future. Remember that the journey to financial stability is ongoing, and staying committed to your financial goals is key to long-term success. Embrace the principles of financial literacy, discipline, and adaptability, and you will be well on your way to a prosperous and fulfilling life.

Thank you for embarking on this journey with us. We wish you all the best in your financial endeavors and hope that this book serves as a valuable resource as you continue to build and sustain your financial independence.

Disclaimer

The information provided in "Rebuilding Financial Stability: A Practical Guide to Debt-Free Living and Future Planning" is for general informational purposes only and is not intended to be financial advice. The content of this book is based on the author's personal experiences, research, and knowledge, and it may not be suitable for all individuals or situations.

Before making any financial decisions or taking any actions based on the information presented in this book, it is highly recommended that you consult with a qualified financial advisor, accountant, or other professional who is aware of your individual circumstances and can provide personalized advice. The author and publisher are not responsible for any financial decisions made by readers based on the content of this book.

Every effort has been made to ensure the accuracy and reliability of the information provided. However, financial regulations, products, and services may change over time, and the author and publisher make no guarantees or warranties regarding the completeness, accuracy, or timeliness of the information contained herein.

By using this book, you acknowledge and agree that the author and publisher shall not be held liable for any losses, damages, or other consequences resulting from your reliance on the information provided. Your use of the information in this book is at your own risk.

CHAPTER 1: UNDERSTANDING YOUR FINANCIAL SITUATION

U nderstanding your financial situation is the first crucial step towards rebuilding financial stability. The economic landscape has dramatically changed post-COVID-19, making it more important than ever to have a clear understanding of your finances. The pandemic has had a profound impact on economies worldwide, leading to job losses, reduced incomes, and increased financial uncertainty. In such times, taking control of your finances can provide a sense of security and peace of mind. This chapter will guide you through assessing your current financial status, setting realistic financial goals, and creating a comprehensive financial plan. By the end of this chapter, you will have a clear understanding of where you stand financially and a roadmap to achieve your financial goals.

1.1: Assessing Your Current Financial Status

Before you can improve your financial situation, you need to understand it fully. Assessing your current financial status involves identifying all your debts and obligations, calculating your net worth, and tracking your income and expenses. This section will provide you with the tools and knowledge to get a clear picture of your financial health.

1.1.1: Listing All Debts and Obligations

To manage your debts effectively, you need to know exactly what you owe. This involves creating a detailed list of all your debts, including credit cards, loans, and personal debts. This process will help you understand your total debt and prioritize your repayment strategy.

- **Identify and Categorize Different Types of Debt**: List all your debts, such as credit card balances, personal loans, car loans, student loans, and any other liabilities. Categorizing your debts helps you see the bigger picture and determine which debts to tackle first.

- **Gather All Statements and Relevant Documents**: Collect all your financial statements, including credit card statements, loan agreements, and any other documents related to your debts. Having all the information in one place makes it easier to manage your repayments.

- **Note Down Interest Rates, Minimum Payments, and Due Dates**: For each debt, write down the interest rate, minimum monthly payment, and due date. This information is crucial for prioritizing which debts to pay off first and understanding the total cost of your debt.

- **Importance of Creating a Debt Inventory**: A debt

inventory is a comprehensive list of all your debts. It helps you see the full extent of your financial obligations and create a plan to manage and pay off your debts systematically.

The post-COVID-19 economic environment has made it clear that managing debt is more important than ever. With rising unemployment rates and economic instability, understanding and controlling your debt can provide a buffer against financial shocks.

Workbook Activity: Debt Inventory Template

Use this template to list all your debts and obligations. This will help you understand your total debt and prioritize your repayment strategy. Include details such as the type of debt, interest rate, minimum payment, and due date.

Debt Type	Interest Rate	Minimum Payment	Due Date	Total Amount
Credit Card				
Personal Loan				
Car Loan				
Student Loan				
Other Debt				

1.1.2: Calculating Your Net Worth

Calculating your net worth is an essential step in understanding your financial health. Your net worth is the difference between your assets and liabilities. This subsection will guide you through the process of listing all your assets and liabilities and calculating your net worth.

- **Definition and Significance of Net Worth**: Net worth is a snapshot of your financial health at a specific point in time. It represents the difference between what you own (assets) and what you owe (liabilities). A positive net worth indicates that you have more assets than liabilities, while a negative net worth means you owe more than you own.

- **Steps to List All Assets**: Include all your financial assets such as cash, savings accounts, retirement accounts, investments, real estate, and any other valuable possessions. This gives you a complete picture of your financial resources.

- **Steps to List All Liabilities**: List all your debts, including credit card balances, loans, mortgages, and any other financial obligations. This helps you understand the total amount of money you owe.

- **Formula to Calculate Net Worth**: The formula for calculating net worth is simple: Net Worth = Total Assets - Total Liabilities. This calculation gives you a clear understanding of your financial position.

- **Examples and Templates for Net Worth Calculation**: Provide examples of how to list assets and liabilities and calculate net worth. Include a template that readers can use to perform their own net worth calculation.

Understanding your net worth is especially important in the current economic climate. The pandemic has shown that financial security can be fragile, and having a clear picture of your net worth can help you make informed decisions about saving, investing, and spending.

Workbook Activity: Net Worth Calculation Template

Use this template to calculate your net worth by listing all your assets and liabilities.

Assets	Amount	Liabilities	Amount
Cash and Savings		Credit Card Debt	
Retirement Accounts		Personal Loans	
Investments		Car Loan	
Real Estate		Mortgage	
Personal Property		Student Loans	
Other Assets		Other Liabilities	

Total Assets		Total Liabilities	
Net Worth (Assets - Liabilities)			

1.1.3: Tracking Your Income and Expenses

Understanding your cash flow is critical for financial stability. Tracking your income and expenses, helps you identify where your money is going and find areas where you can cut costs. This subsection will provide methods and tools for recording your income and monitoring your spending habits.

- **Importance of Understanding Cash Flow**: Cash flow is the movement of money in and out of your accounts. Understanding your cash flow helps you manage your finances more effectively, ensuring you have enough money to cover your expenses and save for the future.

- **Methods to Record All Sources of Income**: Record all your sources of income, including salary, freelance work, investment returns, and any other earnings. This gives you a complete picture of your monthly income.

- **Techniques to Monitor Spending Habits**: Track your expenses by categorizing them into different categories such as housing, transportation, food, entertainment, and savings. This helps you see where your money is going and identify areas where you can cut back.

- **Tools and Apps for Tracking Income and Expenses**: Use financial management tools and apps to track your income and expenses automatically. Apps like Mint, YNAB (You Need A Budget), and PocketGuard can help you manage your finances more effectively.

- **Creating a Monthly Income and Expense Report**: Compile your income and expenses into a monthly report. This report helps you see your financial situation at a glance and make informed decisions about your spending and saving habits.

In the wake of COVID-19, many people have experienced significant changes in their income and expenses. Understanding and adjusting to these changes is essential for maintaining financial stability. By tracking your income and expenses, you can make necessary adjustments to your budget and ensure that you are living within your means.

Workbook Activity: Monthly Income and Expense Tracker

Track your monthly income and expenses to understand your cash flow.

Income Sources	Amount	Expense Categories	Amount
Salary		Housing	
Freelance Work		Transportation	
Investment Returns		Food	
Other Income		Entertainment	
		Savings	
		Other Expenses	
Total Income		**Total Expenses**	
Net Income (Income - Expenses)			

1.2: Setting Financial Goals

Setting financial goals is a vital part of achieving financial stability. This section will help you define both short-term and long-term financial goals and create a plan to achieve them. By setting clear and achievable goals, you can stay motivated and track your progress.

1.2.1: Defining Short-Term Goals

Short-term goals are the stepping-stones to long-term financial stability. These goals should be specific, measurable, achievable, relevant, and time-bound (SMART). This subsection will guide you through the process of setting and planning short-term financial goals.

- **Importance of Short-Term Goals in Financial Planning**: Short-term goals provide immediate direction and motivation. They help you make incremental progress towards larger, long-term objectives.
- **Examples of Short-Term Goals**: Paying off high-interest debt, building an emergency fund, saving for a specific purchase, etc.
- **Setting SMART Goals**: Specific, Measurable, Achievable, Relevant, and Time-bound.
- **Creating an Action Plan for Short-Term Goals**: Break down each goal into actionable steps and set deadlines for each step.

In the current economic climate, setting short-term financial goals can help you navigate uncertainty and build a buffer against financial shocks. Whether it is paying off debt or saving for emergencies, having clear short-term goals can provide a sense of control and direction.

Workbook Activity: Short-Term Goal Setting Template

Use this template to define and plan your short-term financial

goals.

Goal	Specific	Measurable	Achievable	Time-bound

1.2.2: Establishing Long-Term Goals

Long-term goals are essential for achieving overall financial stability and security. These goals often involve significant life events and require careful planning and prioritization. This subsection will help you establish and prioritize your long-term financial goals.

- **Role of Long-Term Goals in Achieving Financial Stability**: Long-term goals provide a vision for your financial future. They help you stay focused and committed to your financial plan.

- **Examples of Long-Term Goals**: Saving for retirement, planning for major life events (buying a house, education), etc.

- **Steps to Prioritize Long-Term Goals**: Evaluate your personal values and needs. Determine which goals are most important and feasible given your financial situation.

- **Developing a Timeline and Strategy for Long-Term Goals**: Create a timeline for achieving each goal and outline the steps needed to reach them.

Setting long-term financial goals is crucial in the post-COVID-19 world. The pandemic has highlighted the importance of financial planning and the need to prepare for unexpected events. By setting long-term goals, you can create a roadmap for your financial future and work towards achieving financial security.

Workbook Activity: Long-Term Goal Setting Template

Use this template to define and plan your long-term financial

goals.

Goal	Specific	Measurable	Achievable	Time-bound

1.3: Creating A Financial Plan

A financial plan is a roadmap to achieving your financial goals. It involves creating a realistic budget, implementing the plan, and seeking professional advice when necessary. This section will provide you with the tools to develop and maintain a comprehensive financial plan.

1.3.1: Developing a Realistic Budget

Creating a budget is a fundamental aspect of financial planning. A well-structured budget helps you allocate your income effectively and manage your expenses. This subsection will guide you through the steps to develop a realistic and comprehensive budget.

- **Importance of Budgeting in Financial Planning**: Budgeting helps you control your spending, save for the future, and avoid debt.
- **Steps to Create a Comprehensive Budget**: Identify your income sources, categorize your expenses, allocate funds for savings and debt repayment, etc.
- **Allocating Income Towards Necessary Expenses, Debt Repayment, Savings, and Discretionary Spending**: Prioritize your spending to ensure you cover essential expenses and work towards your financial goals.
- **Examples of Budget Templates and Tools**: Provide examples of different budgeting methods and tools to help readers create their own budget.

The economic uncertainty following the COVID-19 pandemic has underscored the importance of having a budget. A realistic budget can help you manage your finances, reduce stress, and ensure that you are prepared for any unexpected expenses.

Workbook Activity: Budget Planner Template

Use this template to create your own budget.

Income Source	Amount	Expense Category	Amount
Salary		Housing	
Freelance Work		Transportation	
Investment Returns		Food	
Other Income		Entertainment	
		Savings	
		Other Expenses	
Total Income		Total Expenses	
Net Income (Income - Expenses)			

1.3.2: Implementing the Financial Plan

Once you have a financial plan in place, the next step is to implement it. This involves staying disciplined, regularly reviewing your plan, and making adjustments as needed. This subsection will provide tips and strategies for effectively implementing your financial plan.

- **Starting with Small, Manageable Steps**: Break down your financial plan into smaller, actionable steps that are easy to manage and achieve.

- **Techniques for Staying Disciplined and Committed to the Plan**: Set reminders, track your progress, and reward yourself for reaching milestones.

- **Regularly Reviewing and Adjusting the Financial Plan as Needed**: Periodically review your plan to ensure it remains relevant and make adjustments based on changes in your financial situation.

- **Tracking Progress and Celebrating Milestones**: Keep

track of your progress and celebrate when you reach important milestones to stay motivated.

Implementing a financial plan can be challenging, especially in uncertain times. However, by taking small steps and staying committed, you can achieve your financial goals and build a more secure future.

Workbook Activity: Financial Plan Implementation Checklist

Use this checklist to track your progress and milestones as you implement your financial plan.

Action Item	Completed (Yes/No)

1.3.3: Seeking Professional Advice

Seeking professional financial advice can provide you with personalized guidance and help you make informed decisions. This subsection will discuss the benefits of consulting a financial advisor and how to choose the right one for your needs.

- **Benefits of Consulting a Financial Advisor**: Financial advisors can provide expert advice tailored to your unique financial situation, helping you create and implement a plan to achieve your goals.
- **How to Choose the Right Financial Advisor**: Look for advisors with relevant experience, credentials, and a good reputation. Consider their fee structure and ensure their services align with your needs.
- **Questions to Ask a Financial Advisor**: Ask about their experience, qualifications, approach to financial

planning, and how they can help you achieve your financial goals.

- **Understanding the Costs and Potential Benefits of Financial Advice**: Weigh the costs of hiring a financial advisor against the potential benefits of their advice in helping you achieve financial stability.

In times of economic uncertainty, seeking professional advice can provide valuable insights and help you navigate complex financial decisions. A financial advisor can help you create a robust financial plan and provide ongoing support as you work towards your goals.

Chapter Quiz

1. What is the formula for calculating net worth?
    ◦ Answer: Net Worth = Total Assets - Total Liabilities

2. Why is it important to create a debt inventory?
    ◦ Answer: A debt inventory helps you see the full extent of your financial obligations and create a plan to manage and pay off your debts systematically.

3. Name two methods for tracking income and expenses.
    ◦ Answer: Recording all sources of income and categorizing expenses; using financial management tools and apps like Mint or YNAB.

4. What does the acronym SMART stand for in goal setting?
    ◦ Answer: Specific, Measurable, Achievable, Relevant, Time-bound

Chapter 1: Key Takeaways

1. **Understand Your Financial Situation**: The first step to rebuilding financial stability is to fully understand your current financial status, including all debts, assets, and expenses.

2. **Create a Debt Inventory**: List all your debts, noting down interest rates, minimum payments, and due dates to help prioritize your repayment strategy.

3. **Calculate Your Net Worth**: Determine your net worth by subtracting total liabilities from total assets. This provides a clear snapshot of your financial health.

4. **Track Income and Expenses**: Regularly track your income and categorize your expenses to identify areas for potential savings and to maintain a balanced budget.

5. **Set SMART Financial Goals**: Define short-term and long-term financial goals that are Specific, Measurable, Achievable, Relevant, and Time-bound.

6. **Develop a Realistic Budget**: Create and maintain a budget that allocates income towards essential expenses, debt repayment, savings, and discretionary spending.

7. **Implement and Adjust Your Financial Plan**: Stay disciplined in following your financial plan, regularly review your progress, and adjust the plan as necessary.

8. **Seek Professional Financial Advice**: Consider consulting a financial advisor for personalized guidance and support in achieving your financial goals.

9. **Adapt to Economic Changes**: Be mindful of the current economic conditions, such as those influenced by the COVID-19 pandemic, and adjust your financial

strategies accordingly.

10. **Maintain Financial Discipline and Motivation**: Stay committed to your financial plan, track progress, and celebrate milestones to keep yourself motivated.

CHAPTER 2: BUILDING A SOLID FINANCIAL FOUNDATION

Now that you have a clear understanding of your current financial situation, it is time to build a solid financial foundation. This foundation will support you as you work towards your financial goals and ensure that you are prepared for unexpected challenges. In Chapter 1, we focused on assessing your financial status, setting goals, and creating a financial plan. Chapter 2 will take these principles further, helping you to develop habits and strategies that will strengthen your financial health over the long term.

We will explore the importance of emergency funds, insurance, and investments. These elements are crucial in protecting your financial well-being and ensuring that you can weather financial storms. We will also discuss ways to increase your income and manage your expenses effectively, ensuring that you have a strong base to build upon.

2.1: Establishing An Emergency Fund

One of the most important steps in building a solid financial foundation is establishing an emergency fund. This fund acts as a financial safety net, providing you with the resources to handle unexpected expenses without derailing your financial plan.

2.1.1: Importance of an Emergency Fund

An emergency fund is crucial for financial stability. It can help you cover unexpected expenses such as medical bills, car repairs, or job loss. Without an emergency fund, you may be forced to rely on credit cards or loans, which can lead to increased debt and financial stress.

- **Protection Against Unexpected Expenses**: An emergency fund provides a buffer against unexpected financial shocks, helping you avoid debt.
- **Peace of Mind**: Knowing that you have a safety net can reduce financial stress and help you focus on other financial goals.
- **Flexibility and Security**: Having an emergency fund gives you the flexibility to handle emergencies without compromising your financial stability.

2.1.2: Determining the Right Amount for Your Emergency Fund

The amount you need in your emergency fund depends on your personal circumstances, such as your income, expenses, and dependents. A general rule of thumb is to save three to six months' worth of living expenses.

- **Assessing Your Monthly Expenses**: Calculate your average monthly expenses, including rent/mortgage, utilities, food, transportation, and other necessities.
- **Setting a Savings Goal**: Based on your monthly expenses, determine a realistic savings goal for your emergency fund.
- **Building Your Fund Gradually**: Start by saving a small amount each month and gradually increase your contributions until you reach your goal.

Workbook Activity: Emergency Fund Calculation Template

Use this template to calculate the amount you need in your

emergency fund.

Monthly Expense Category	Amount
Housing	
Utilities	
Food	
Transportation	
Insurance	
Other Essentials	
Total Monthly Expenses	
Emergency Fund Goal (3-6 months of expenses)	

2.1.3: Strategies for Building Your Emergency Fund

Building an emergency fund requires discipline and consistency. This subsection will provide strategies to help you save effectively.

- **Automate Your Savings**: Set up automatic transfers to your emergency fund to ensure consistent savings.
- **Cut Unnecessary Expenses**: Identify and reduce discretionary spending to free up more money for your emergency fund.
- **Use Windfalls Wisely**: Allocate bonuses, tax refunds, or other unexpected income to your emergency fund.

Workbook Activity: Emergency Fund Savings Plan

Create a plan to build your emergency fund, including monthly savings goals and strategies to increase your savings.

2.2: Protecting Your Financial Well-Being With Insurance

Insurance is a critical component of a solid financial foundation. It protects you and your assets from unexpected events that could otherwise lead to significant financial hardship. This section will explore the different types of insurance you need and how to choose the right policies for your needs.

2.2.1: Types of Essential Insurance

Different types of insurance provide coverage for various aspects of your life. This subsection will cover the essential types of insurance you should consider.

- **Health Insurance**: Covers medical expenses, reducing the financial burden of healthcare costs.
- **Auto Insurance**: Provides coverage for vehicle-related accidents and damages.
- **Homeowners/Renters Insurance**: Protects your home and personal belongings against theft, damage, and natural disasters.
- **Life Insurance**: Offers financial protection to your dependents in the event of your death.
- **Disability Insurance**: Provides income replacement if you are unable to work due to illness or injury.

2.2.2: Evaluating Your Insurance Needs

Determining the right amount and type of insurance coverage involves assessing your personal situation and potential risks.

- **Assessing Your Risk Factors**: Consider factors such as health, occupation, and lifestyle when evaluating your insurance needs.
- **Choosing Appropriate Coverage Levels**: Ensure you have sufficient coverage to protect against significant financial loss.
- **Comparing Insurance Policies**: Shop around and compare policies to find the best coverage at an affordable price.

Workbook Activity: Insurance Needs Assessment Template

Use this template to evaluate your insurance needs and determine the appropriate coverage levels.

Insurance Type	Current Coverage	Recommended Coverage	Notes
Health			

Insurance			
Auto Insurance			
Homeowners/ Renters Insurance			
Life Insurance			
Disability Insurance			

2.2.3: Understanding Insurance Policies and Terms

Insurance policies can be complex and filled with jargon. This subsection will help you understand key terms and provisions.

- **Premiums and Deductibles**: Understand the cost of your insurance policy and the amount you must pay out-of-pocket before coverage begins.

- **Coverage Limits and Exclusions**: Know the maximum amount your insurance will pay and any exclusions to coverage.

- **Claims Process**: Learn how to file a claim and what to expect during the process.

2.3: Building Wealth Through Investments

Investing is an essential part of building long-term wealth and achieving financial stability. This section will introduce you to the basics of investing and provide strategies for building a diversified investment portfolio.

2.3.1: Understanding Investment Basics

Investing involves putting your money to work to generate returns over time. This subsection will cover the fundamental concepts of investing.

- **Types of Investments**: Explore different investment options, including stocks, bonds, mutual funds, real estate, and more.

- **Risk and Return**: Understand the relationship

between risk and potential return, and how to balance them in your portfolio.

.   **Time Horizon and Investment Goals**: Determine your investment time frame and goals to choose appropriate investments.

2.3.2: Building a Diversified Investment Portfolio

Diversification is key to managing investment risk. This subsection will guide you in creating a diversified portfolio that aligns with your financial goals.

.   **Asset Allocation**: Distribute your investments across different asset classes to reduce risk.

.   **Choosing Investments**: Select specific investments within each asset class based on your risk tolerance and goals.

.   **Rebalancing Your Portfolio**: Regularly review and adjust your portfolio to maintain your desired asset allocation.

Workbook Activity: Investment Portfolio Template

Use this template to create a diversified investment portfolio.

Asset Class	Target Allocation (%)	Current Allocation (%)	Actions Needed
Stocks			
Bonds			
Real Estate			
Cash and Equivalents			
Other Investments			

2.3.3: Investment Strategies for Different Life Stages

Your investment strategy should evolve as you move through different stages of life. This subsection will provide guidance on how to adjust your investments based on your age and financial

goals.

- **Young Professionals**: Focus on growth-oriented investments to build wealth over time.
- **Mid-Career**: Balance growth and stability as you prepare for major life events like buying a home or funding education.
- **Pre-Retirement**: Shift towards more conservative investments to protect your wealth as you approach retirement.
- **Retirement**: Generate income and preserve capital to support your retirement lifestyle.

Workbook Activity: Life Stage Investment Plan

Create an investment plan tailored to your current life stage and future financial goals.

2.4: Increasing Your Income And Managing Expenses

Increasing your income and managing your expenses effectively are crucial steps in building a strong financial foundation. This section will explore strategies to boost your earnings and control your spending.

2.4.1: Strategies to Increase Your Income

Finding ways to increase your income can help you reach your financial goals faster. This subsection will provide various strategies to boost your earnings.

- **Advancing in Your Career**: Seek promotions, additional responsibilities, or advanced education to increase your earning potential.
- **Side Hustles and Freelancing**: Explore opportunities to earn extra income through side jobs or freelance work.
- **Passive Income Streams**: Invest in assets that generate

passive income, such as rental properties or dividend-paying stocks.

2.4.2: Effective Expense Management

Managing your expenses effectively ensures that you live within your means and save more for your financial goals. This subsection will offer tips for controlling your spending.

- **Creating a Spending Plan**: Develop a detailed plan for how you will spend your income each month.
- **Identifying and Reducing Unnecessary Expenses**: Review your expenses regularly and eliminate or reduce non-essential spending.
- **Using Budgeting Tools and Apps**: Utilize tools and apps to track your spending and stay on budget.

Workbook Activity: Income and Expense Plan

Create a plan to increase your income and manage your expenses effectively.

Income Source	Current Amount	Target Amount	Actions Needed
Salary			
Freelance Work			
Passive Income			
Total Income			

Expense Category	Current Amount	Target Amount	Actions Needed
Housing			
Utilities			
Food			
Transportation			
Entertainment			
Savings			

Other Expenses			
Total Expenses			

Chapter Quiz

1. Why is establishing an emergency fund important for financial stability?
   - Answer: An emergency fund provides a buffer against unexpected financial shocks, helping you avoid debt and providing peace of mind.

2. What are the key types of insurance everyone should consider?
   - Answer: Health insurance, auto insurance, homeowners/renters insurance, life insurance, and disability insurance.

3. Why is diversification important in an investment portfolio?
   - Answer: Diversification helps manage investment risk by spreading investments across different asset classes.

4. What are some strategies to increase your income?
   - Answer: Advancing in your career, side hustles and freelancing, and generating passive income streams.

5. How can effective expense management contribute to financial stability?
   - Answer: Effective expense management ensures you live within your means and save more for your financial goals.

Chapter 2: Key Takeaways

1. **Establish an Emergency Fund**: Create a financial safety net to cover unexpected expenses and provide peace of mind.

2. **Protect Your Financial Well-being with Insurance**: Ensure you have adequate insurance coverage to protect against significant financial losses.

3. **Build Wealth Through Investments**: Develop a diversified investment portfolio that aligns with your financial goals and risk tolerance.

4. **Increase Your Income**: Explore strategies to boost your earnings, including advancing in your career, side hustles, and passive income streams.

5. **Manage Your Expenses Effectively**: Create a spending plan, reduce unnecessary expenses, and use budgeting tools to stay on track.

With a solid financial foundation in place, it is time to explore strategies for debt repayment and management. In Chapter 3, we will delve into the various methods to effectively reduce and manage debt, ensuring that you remain on track towards achieving financial stability. We will discuss the snowball and avalanche methods, consolidating debt, and negotiating with creditors. By the end of Chapter 3, you will have a clear plan for tackling your debts and moving closer to financial freedom.

CHAPTER 3:
EFFECTIVE DEBT
REPAYMENT AND
MANAGEMENT
STRATEGIES

With a solid financial foundation established, it is now time to tackle one of the most critical aspects of financial stability: debt repayment and management. In Chapter 1, we assessed your financial situation and identified your debts. In Chapter 2, we built a strong financial foundation to support your financial goals. Chapter 3 will focus on strategies to effectively reduce and manage your debt, ensuring that you stay on track towards achieving financial freedom.

We will explore various methods for debt repayment, including the snowball and avalanche methods. We will also discuss options for consolidating debt, negotiating with creditors, and the psychological aspects of managing debt. By the end of this chapter, you will have a comprehensive plan for tackling your debts and moving closer to financial independence.

3.1: Understanding Debt Repayment Strategies

Effective debt repayment requires a strategic approach. This section will introduce you to two popular methods for paying off debt: the snowball method and the avalanche method. Each method has its advantages and can be tailored to your personal financial situation.

3.1.1: The Snowball Method

The snowball method focuses on paying off your smallest debts first, gradually working your way up to larger debts. This method can provide a psychological boost by allowing you to see progress quickly.

- **How the Snowball Method Works**: List your debts from smallest to largest. Pay the minimum on all debts except the smallest, which you pay off as quickly as possible. Once the smallest debt is paid off, move to the next smallest debt, and so on.
- **Advantages of the Snowball Method**: Provides quick wins and boosts motivation, making it easier to stay committed to your debt repayment plan.
- **Steps to Implement the Snowball Method**:
  - List your debts from smallest to largest.
  - Allocate extra funds to the smallest debt while making minimum payments on others.
  - Repeat the process as each debt is paid off.

Workbook Activity: Snowball Method Debt Repayment Plan

Use this template to create a debt repayment plan using the snowball method.

Debt Type	Balance	Minimum Payment	Extra Payment	New Balance
Smallest Debt				
Next Smallest				

Larger Debt				
Largest Debt				

3.1.2: The Avalanche Method

The avalanche method prioritizes paying off debts with the highest interest rates first. This method can save you money in interest payments over time.

- **How the Avalanche Method Works**: List your debts from highest to lowest interest rate. Pay the minimum on all debts except the one with the highest interest rate, which you pay off as quickly as possible. Once the highest-interest debt is paid off, move to the next highest, and so on.

- **Advantages of the Avalanche Method**: Reduces the total amount of interest paid over the life of the debt, potentially saving you money.

- **Steps to Implement the Avalanche Method**:
  - List your debts from highest to lowest interest rate.
  - Allocate extra funds to the highest-interest debt while making minimum payments on others.
  - Repeat the process as each high-interest debt is paid off.

Workbook Activity: Avalanche Method Debt Repayment Plan

Use this template to create a debt repayment plan using the avalanche method.

Debt Type	Balance	Interest Rate	Minimum Payment	Extra Payment	New Balance
Highest Interest					
Next Highest					
Lower Interest					
Lowest Interest					

3.2: Debt Consolidation And Refinancing

Debt consolidation and refinancing are strategies that can simplify your debt repayment process and potentially reduce your interest rates. This section will explore these options and help you determine if they are right for you.

3.2.1: What is Debt Consolidation?

Debt consolidation involves combining multiple debts into a single loan or payment. This can make managing your debt easier and may reduce your overall interest rate.

- **How Debt Consolidation Works**: Combine multiple debts into a single loan with a lower interest rate or more manageable payment terms.

- **Types of Debt Consolidation**: Personal loans, balance transfer credit cards, home equity loans, and debt management plans.

- **Advantages and Disadvantages**: Simplifies payments, potentially lowers interest rates, but may come with fees and require good credit.

Workbook Activity: Debt Consolidation Evaluation

Evaluate whether debt consolidation is a suitable option for you.

Debt Type	Balance	Interest Rate	Consolidation Option	New Interest Rate	Fees	Savings
Debt 1						
Debt 2						
Debt 3						
Total Savings						

3.2.2: Refinancing Debt

Refinancing involves replacing an existing loan with a new one, typically with better terms. This can be a useful strategy for reducing interest rates and monthly payments.

- **How Refinancing Works**: Apply for a new loan to pay off an existing loan, ideally with a lower interest rate or better terms.

- **When to Consider Refinancing**: Interest rates have dropped, your credit score has improved, or you need to lower your monthly payments.

- **Steps to Refinance Your Debt**:
  - Research and compare refinancing options.
  - Apply for a new loan and use it to pay off your existing debt.
  - Adjust your budget to accommodate new payment terms.

Workbook Activity: Refinancing Evaluation

Evaluate whether refinancing your debt is a suitable option for you.

Current Loan	Balance	Interest Rate	New Loan Option	New Interest Rate	Monthly Payment	Savings
Loan 1						
Loan 2						
Loan 3						
Total Savings						

3.3: Negotiating With Creditors

Negotiating with your creditors can help you manage your debt more effectively by potentially reducing your interest rates, monthly payments, or overall debt balance. This section will provide strategies for successfully negotiating with creditors.

3.3.1: Preparing for Negotiation

Effective negotiation requires preparation. This subsection will guide you through the steps to prepare for a successful negotiation with your creditors.

- **Assess Your Financial Situation**: Understand your income, expenses, and debt obligations before negotiating.
- **Research Your Options**: Know what options are available, such as lower interest rates, extended payment terms, or debt settlement.
- **Gather Documentation**: Collect all relevant financial documents, including pay stubs, bank statements, and debt statements.

3.3.2: Strategies for Negotiating with Creditors

Negotiating with creditors can be challenging, but these strategies can increase your chances of success.

- **Be Honest and Transparent**: Clearly explain your financial situation and why you need assistance.
- **Propose a Solution** Offer a realistic repayment plan that you can afford.
- **Stay Calm and Professional**: Approach the negotiation with a calm and professional demeanor.
- **Get Agreements in Writing**: Ensure any agreements made are documented in writing.

Workbook Activity: Creditor Negotiation Plan

Create a plan for negotiating with your creditors, including key points to discuss and proposed solutions.

Creditor	Current Balance	Current Terms	Proposed Terms	Notes
Creditor 1				
Creditor 2				
Creditor 3				

3.4: Psychological Aspects Of Managing Debt

Managing debt can be a stressful and emotionally challenging process. Understanding the psychological aspects of debt management can help you stay motivated and maintain a positive mindset. This section will provide strategies for coping with the emotional challenges of debt.

3.4.1: Dealing with Debt-Related Stress

Debt-related stress can affect your mental and physical health. This subsection will explore ways to manage and reduce stress related to debt.

- **Recognize the Signs of Stress**: Identify symptoms of stress, such as anxiety, irritability, and difficulty sleeping.

- **Practice Stress-Reduction Techniques**: Engage in activities that reduce stress, such as exercise, meditation, and deep breathing exercises.
- **Seek Support**: Talk to friends, family, or a financial counselor for support and guidance.

3.4.2: Staying Motivated

Staying motivated throughout the debt repayment process can be challenging. This subsection will provide tips for maintaining motivation and celebrating progress.

- **Set Milestones and Rewards**: Break your debt repayment plan into smaller milestones and reward yourself when you reach them.
- **Visualize Your Progress**: Use visual aids, such as charts and graphs, to track your progress and stay motivated.
- **Focus on the End Goal**: Keep your long-term financial goals in mind to stay motivated and committed to your debt repayment plan.

Workbook Activity: Stress Management and Motivation Plan

Create a plan to manage stress and stay motivated during your debt repayment journey.

Stress-Reduction Techniques	Frequency	Notes
Exercise		
Meditation		
Deep Breathing Exercises		
Other		

Milestone	Reward	Notes
Pay off first debt		
Reduce total debt by 25%		
Reduce total debt by 50%		
Pay off all debt		

Chapter Quiz

1. What are the key differences between the snowball and avalanche methods of debt repayment?
    ◦ Answer: The snowball method focuses on paying off the smallest debts first, providing quick wins and motivation. The avalanche method prioritizes paying off debts with the highest interest rates first, potentially saving more money on interest over time.

2. When might debt consolidation be a beneficial strategy?
    ◦ Answer: Debt consolidation can be beneficial if it simplifies payments, reduces interest rates, or provides more manageable payment terms.

3. What are some key steps to take when negotiating with creditors?
    ◦ Answer: Assess your financial situation, research your options, gather documentation, be honest and transparent, propose a solution, stay calm and professional, and get agreements in writing.

4. How can you manage debt-related stress?
    ◦ Answer: Recognize the signs of stress, practice stress-reduction techniques, seek support, and maintain a positive mindset.

5. What are some strategies to stay motivated during the debt repayment process?
    ◦ Answer: Set milestones and rewards, visualize your progress, and focus on your long-term financial goals.

Chapter 3: Key Takeaways

1. **Understand Debt Repayment Strategies**: Learn about the snowball and avalanche methods and choose the one that best suits your financial situation.

2. **Consider Debt Consolidation and Refinancing**: Evaluate these options to simplify your debt repayment process and potentially reduce interest rates.

3. **Negotiate with Creditors**: Use effective negotiation strategies to seek better terms and manage your debt more effectively.

4. **Manage Debt-Related Stress**: Recognize and address the psychological aspects of debt management to maintain your mental and emotional well-being.

5. **Stay Motivated**: Set milestones, visualize progress, and focus on your long-term financial goals to stay committed to your debt repayment plan.

With a solid debt repayment and management plan in place, it is time to focus on building and improving your credit score. In Chapter 4, we will explore the importance of credit scores, how they are calculated, and strategies to improve and maintain a healthy credit score. A strong credit score will not only help you secure better financial products and services but also pave the way for greater financial opportunities in the future.

CHAPTER 4: BUILDING AND IMPROVING YOUR CREDIT SCORE

A healthy credit score is a critical component of financial stability. It can influence your ability to secure loans, obtain favorable interest rates, and access various financial products. In Chapter 3, we focused on effective debt repayment and management strategies. Now, in Chapter 4, we will explore the importance of credit scores, how they are calculated, and the steps you can take to improve and maintain a strong credit score. By understanding and managing your credit score, you can enhance your financial health and open the door to greater financial opportunities.

4.1: Understanding Credit Scores

A credit score is a numerical representation of your creditworthiness. Lenders use this score to assess the risk of lending you money. This section will explain what a credit score is, how it is calculated, and why it is important.

4.1.1: What is a Credit Score?

A credit score is a three-digit number that summarizes your

credit risk. It is based on your credit history and used by lenders to determine your eligibility for loans and credit.

- **Definition of a Credit Score**: A numerical value that represents your creditworthiness, typically ranging from 300 to 850.
- **Importance of a Credit Score**: A higher credit score can lead to better loan terms, lower interest rates, and increased access to credit.
- **Different Credit Scoring Models**: The most commonly used credit scoring models are FICO and VantageScore.

4.1.2: How is a Credit Score Calculated?

Credit scores are calculated based on several factors from your credit report. Understanding these factors can help you manage and improve your score.

- **Payment History (35%)**: Your record of on-time payments is the most significant factor in your credit score.
- **Amounts Owed (30%)**: The total amount of debt you owe and your credit utilization ratio.
- **Length of Credit History (15%)**: The age of your credit accounts and the average length of time they have been open.
- **Credit Mix (10%)**: The variety of credit accounts you have, such as credit cards, mortgages, and auto loans.
- **New Credit (10%)**: The number of recently opened credit accounts and recent inquiries into your credit report.

Workbook Activity: Credit Score Calculation Breakdown

Analyze how each factor contributes to your credit score and identify areas for improvement.

Factor	Percentage	Current Status	Improvement Steps
Payment History	35%		
Amounts Owed	30%		

Length of Credit History	15%		
Credit Mix	10%		
New Credit	10%		

4.1.3: Why is a Good Credit Score Important?

A good credit score can have a significant impact on your financial life. This subsection will explore the benefits of maintaining a high credit score.

- **Lower Interest Rates**: Higher credit scores typically qualify for lower interest rates on loans and credit cards.

- **Better Loan Terms**: Lenders may offer more favorable terms, such as higher credit limits and longer repayment periods.

- **Increased Access to Credit**: A good credit score can make it easier to obtain loans, mortgages, and other financial products.

- **Financial Security**: A strong credit score can provide peace of mind and financial flexibility.

4.2: Steps To Improve Your Credit Score

Improving your credit score requires consistent effort and good financial habits. This section will provide practical steps to help you raise your credit score over time.

4.2.1: Check Your Credit Report Regularly

Regularly checking your credit report can help you identify errors and monitor your progress. This subsection will explain how to obtain and review your credit report.

- **How to Obtain Your Credit Report**: You can request a free credit report annually from each of the three major credit bureaus (Equifax, Experian, and TransUnion) through AnnualCreditReport.com.

- **Reviewing Your Credit Report**: Check for errors, such

as incorrect account information or late payments that were reported inaccurately.

- **Disputing Errors**: If you find errors, dispute them with the credit bureau to have them corrected.

Workbook Activity: Credit Report Checklist

Use this checklist to review your credit report for errors and areas of improvement.

Item	Status	Notes
Personal Information	Accurate	
Account Information	Accurate	
Payment History	Accurate	
Credit Inquiries	Accurate	
Dispute Errors		

4.2.2: Pay Your Bills on Time

Consistently paying your bills on time is crucial for maintaining a good credit score. This subsection will provide tips for ensuring timely payments.

- **Set Up Payment Reminders**: Use calendar reminders, apps, or automatic payments to ensure you never miss a payment.

- **Prioritize On-Time Payments**: Make on-time payments a priority, as late payments can significantly affect your credit score.

- **Manage Due Dates**: If your due dates are inconvenient, contact your creditors to request a change.

4.2.3: Reduce Your Debt

Reducing your debt can improve your credit utilization ratio and positively affect your credit score. This subsection will offer strategies for paying down debt.

- **Pay More Than the Minimum**: Whenever possible, pay more than the minimum payment on your credit accounts.

- **Focus on High-Interest Debt**: Prioritize paying off

high-interest debt to reduce the total amount of interest paid.

- **Avoid New Debt**: Limit new credit applications and focus on paying down existing debt.

Workbook Activity: Debt Reduction Plan

Create a plan to reduce your debt and improve your credit utilization ratio.

Debt Type	Balance	Interest Rate	Minimum Payment	Extra Payment	New Balance
High-Interest Debt					
Next Debt					
Lower Interest					
Lowest Interest					

4.2.4: Increase Your Credit Limit

Increasing your credit limit can improve your credit utilization ratio, provided you do not increase your spending. This subsection will explain how to request a credit limit increase.

- **Requesting a Credit Limit Increase**: Contact your credit card issuer to request a higher credit limit. Be prepared to provide information about your income and employment.

- **Maintaining Low Utilization**: Ensure that your spending does not increase with the higher credit limit to maximize the benefits.

- **Timing Your Request**: Request a credit limit increase after demonstrating responsible credit use for several months.

4.2.5: Diversify Your Credit Mix

Having a variety of credit accounts can positively affect your credit score. This subsection will discuss ways to diversify your credit mix.

- **Types of Credit Accounts**: Examples include credit cards, installment loans (e.g., car loans, mortgages), and retail accounts.

- **Adding New Credit Types**: Consider adding a new type

of credit account if it fits your financial situation and goals.

. **Responsible Use of New Credit**: Use new credit accounts responsibly to avoid increasing your debt.

Workbook Activity: Credit Improvement Plan

Create a comprehensive plan to improve your credit score by addressing key areas.

Action Item	Steps to Take	Timeline
Check Credit Report	Request report and review for errors	Monthly
Pay Bills on Time	Set up reminders and automatic payments	Ongoing
Reduce Debt	Pay more than minimum, focus on high-interest	Ongoing
Increase Credit Limit	Request increase, maintain low utilization	Every 6-12 months
Diversify Credit Mix	Add new credit type responsibly	As needed

4.3: Maintaining A Healthy Credit Score

Once you have improved your credit score, it is important to maintain it. This section will provide tips for sustaining a healthy credit score over the long term.

4.3.1: Monitor Your Credit Regularly

Regularly monitoring your credit can help you stay on top of your financial health and quickly address any issues.

. **Credit Monitoring Services**: Consider using credit-monitoring services to receive alerts about changes to your credit report.

. **Regular Check-Ins**: Schedule regular check-ins to review your credit report and ensure everything is accurate.

. **Addressing Issues Promptly**: Act quickly to resolve any issues or discrepancies that appear on your credit report.

4.3.2: Practice Responsible Credit Use

Responsible credit use is key to maintaining a good credit score. This subsection will provide tips for using credit wisely.

- **Avoiding High Balances**: Keep your credit card balances low to maintain a good credit utilization ratio.
- **Making Timely Payments**: Continue to make all payments on time, every time.
- **Limiting New Credit Applications**: Only apply for new credit when necessary to avoid hard inquiries that can affect your score.

4.3.3: Plan for the Future

Planning for future financial goals can help you maintain a healthy credit score. This subsection will discuss how to incorporate your credit management into long-term financial planning.

- **Setting Financial Goals**: Include maintaining a healthy credit score as part of your overall financial goals.
- **Saving for Large Purchases**: Save for large purchases to avoid relying on credit.
- **Building an Emergency Fund**: Ensure you have an emergency fund to cover unexpected expenses and avoid accruing new debt.

Workbook Activity: Credit Maintenance Plan

Develop a plan to maintain your improved credit score over time.

Action Item	Steps to Take	Timeline
Monitor Credit	Use monitoring services, check regularly	Monthly
Practice Responsible Credit Use	Avoid high balances, make timely payments	Ongoing
Plan for Future	Set goals, save for	Ongoing

	large purchases, build emergency fund	

Chapter Quiz

1. What factors contribute to your credit score, and how are they weighted?

    ◦ Answer: Payment History (35%), Amounts Owed (30%), Length of Credit History (15%), Credit Mix (10%), New Credit (10%).

2. How can regularly checking your credit report help improve your credit score?

    ◦ Answer: It allows you to identify and correct errors, monitor progress, and ensure accurate information.

3. What are some strategies for reducing your debt and improving your credit utilization ratio?

    ◦ Answer: Pay more than the minimum, focus on high-interest debt, avoid new debt, and request a credit limit increase.

4. Why is it important to maintain a low credit utilization ratio?

    ◦ Answer: It positively affects your credit score by showing you are not overly reliant on credit.

5. How can diversifying your credit mix benefit your credit score?

    ◦ Answer: It shows lenders you can manage different types of credit responsibly.

Chapter 4: Key Takeaways

1. **Understand Credit Scores**: Learn what a credit score is, how it is calculated, and why it is important.

2. **Check Your Credit Report Regularly**: Regularly review your credit report for errors and areas of improvement.

3. **Pay Your Bills on Time**: Consistently make on-time payments to positively affect your credit score.

4. **Reduce Your Debt**: Focus on paying down high-interest debt and avoid accruing new debt.

5. **Increase Your Credit Limit and Diversify Credit Mix**: Improve your credit utilization ratio and manage different types of credit responsibly.

6. **Maintain a Healthy Credit Score**: Monitor your credit regularly, practice responsible credit use, and plan for future financial goals.

With a strong credit score and effective debt management strategies in place, it is time to focus on building long-term wealth through investing. In Chapter 5, we will explore different types of investments, how to create a diversified investment portfolio, and strategies for growing your wealth over time. By understanding and implementing sound investment principles, you can secure your financial future and achieve your long-term financial goals.

CHAPTER 5: BUILDING LONG-TERM WEALTH THROUGH INVESTING

Investing is a powerful tool for building long-term wealth and achieving financial stability. With a strong financial foundation, effective debt management, and a healthy credit score established in previous chapters, you are now ready to explore the world of investing. This chapter will provide an in-depth look at different types of investments, how to create a diversified investment portfolio, and strategies for growing your wealth over time. By understanding and implementing sound investment principles, you can secure your financial future and achieve your long-term financial goals.

5.1: Understanding Different Types Of Investments

There are various types of investments available, each with its own risk and return profile. Understanding these investment options is crucial for building a diversified portfolio that aligns with your financial goals and risk tolerance.

5.1.1: Stocks

Stocks represent ownership in a company and offer the potential for high returns, but they also come with higher risk.

- **What Are Stocks?** Shares of ownership in a company that entitle the shareholder to a portion of the company's profits.
- **Types of Stocks**: Common stocks and preferred stocks.
- **Risks and Returns**: Stocks can offer high returns, but they are also subject to market volatility and company-specific risks.

Workbook Activity: Stock Investment Analysis

Analyze a few stocks of interest by examining their historical performance, financial health, and market position.

Stock Name	Ticker Symbol	Industry	Historical Performance	Financial Health	Market Position

5.1.2: Bonds

Bonds are debt securities issued by governments or corporations that provide fixed interest payments over a specified period.

- **What Are Bonds?** Loans made to a corporation or government in exchange for periodic interest payments and the return of principal at maturity.
- **Types of Bonds**: Government bonds, corporate bonds, municipal bonds, and high-yield bonds.
- **Risks and Returns**: Bonds generally offer lower returns than stocks but come with lower risk. Interest rate changes and credit risk are key considerations.

Workbook Activity: Bond Investment Analysis

Evaluate a few bonds based on their interest rates, credit ratings, and maturity dates.

Bond Name	Issuer	Type	Interest Rate	Credit Rating	Maturity Date

5.1.3: Mutual Funds and Exchange-Traded Funds (ETFs)

Mutual funds and ETFs pool money from many investors to invest in a diversified portfolio of stocks, bonds, or other securities.

- **What Are Mutual Funds and ETFs?** Investment funds that allow investors to buy shares representing a portion of the fund's holdings.

- **Types of Mutual Funds and ETFs**: Equity funds, bond funds, index funds, sector funds, and international funds.

- **Risks and Returns**: Diversified exposure reduces individual security risk, but market risk remains. Fees and expenses can affect returns.

Workbook Activity: Mutual Fund and ETF Analysis

Compare a few mutual funds and ETFs based on their performance, expense ratios, and portfolio composition.

Fund Name	Type	Performance	Expense Ratio	Portfolio Composition

5.1.4: Real Estate

Real estate investing involves purchasing property to generate income or appreciation.

- **What Is Real Estate Investing?** Acquiring property for rental income, capital appreciation, or both.

- **Types of Real Estate Investments**: Residential properties, commercial properties, real estate investment trusts (REITs).

- **Risks and Returns**: Real estate can provide steady income and potential appreciation but involves high upfront costs, ongoing maintenance, and market risk.

Workbook Activity: Real Estate Investment Analysis

Evaluate potential real estate investments based on location, property type, rental income potential, and market trends.

Property Type	Location	Purchase Price	Rental Income Potential	Market Trends

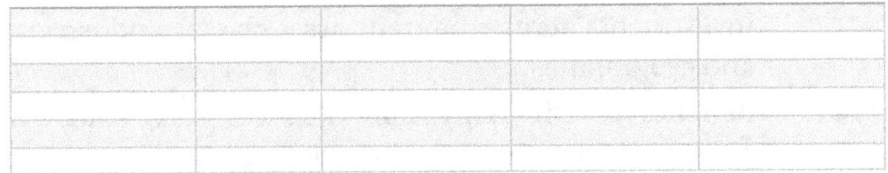

5.1.5: Alternative Investments

Alternative investments include assets outside traditional stocks, bonds, and real estate.

- **What Are Alternative Investments?** Assets such as commodities, hedge funds, private equity, and collectibles.
- **Types of Alternative Investments**: Gold, silver, oil, hedge funds, private equity, art, and collectibles.
- **Risks and Returns**: Alternative investments can offer diversification benefits and potential high returns but often come with higher risk, lower liquidity, and higher fees.

Workbook Activity: Alternative Investment Analysis

Explore a few alternative investments, considering their potential returns, risks, and role in a diversified portfolio.

Investment Type	Description	Potential Returns	Risks	Liquidity

5.2: Creating A Diversified Investment Portfolio

Diversification is key to managing investment risk. This section will guide you in creating a diversified investment portfolio that aligns with your financial goals and risk tolerance.

5.2.1: Importance of Diversification

Diversification spreads investment risk across various assets, reducing the impact of any single investment's poor performance.

- **What Is Diversification?** The practice of spreading

investments across different asset classes, industries, and geographies.

- **Benefits of Diversification**: Reduces risk, smooths returns, and enhances the potential for long-term growth.
- **Challenges of Diversification**: Requires knowledge and management to balance the portfolio and avoid over-diversification.

5.2.2: Asset Allocation

Asset allocation is the process of deciding how to distribute your investments among different asset classes.

- **What Is Asset Allocation?** The distribution of investments across various asset classes such as stocks, bonds, real estate, and cash.
- **Factors Influencing Asset Allocation**: Risk tolerance, investment goals, time horizon, and market conditions.
- **Common Asset Allocation Models**: Conservative, balanced, and aggressive portfolios.

Workbook Activity: Asset Allocation Plan

Create an asset allocation plan based on your risk tolerance and financial goals.

Asset Class	Target Allocation (%)	Current Allocation (%)	Actions Needed
Stocks			
Bonds			
Real Estate			
Cash and Equivalents			
Alternative Investments			

5.2.3: Building and Managing Your Portfolio

Building a diversified portfolio involves selecting the right mix of investments and managing them over time.

- **Steps to Build a Portfolio**:
  - Define your investment goals and risk

tolerance.

- ◦ Choose an asset allocation model.
- ◦ Select specific investments within each asset class.
- ◦ Monitor and rebalance your portfolio regularly.

- **Portfolio Management Strategies**:
  - ◦ Active vs. Passive Management: Active management involves frequent trading to outperform the market, while passive management involves holding investments to match market performance.
  - ◦ Rebalancing: Periodically adjust your portfolio to maintain your desired asset allocation.

Workbook Activity: Portfolio Construction and Management Plan

Develop a plan to build and manage your investment portfolio.

Step	Description	Timeline
Define Goals and Risk Tolerance	Assess financial goals and risk tolerance	Initial Planning
Choose Asset Allocation	Determine target asset allocation	Initial Planning
Select Investments	Research and choose specific investments	Initial Planning
Monitor Portfolio	Regularly review and adjust investments	Monthly/Quarterly
Rebalance Portfolio	Adjust asset allocation as needed	Annually/Semi-Annually

5.3: Strategies For Growing Your Wealth Over Time

Growing your wealth requires a combination of sound investment strategies, disciplined saving, and ongoing financial education. This section will explore various strategies for building long-term wealth.

5.3.1: Dollar-Cost Averaging

Dollar-cost averaging involves investing a fixed amount of money at regular intervals, regardless of market conditions.

- **What Is Dollar-Cost Averaging?** A strategy that involves consistently investing a fixed amount of money in the market, reducing the impact of market volatility.
- **Benefits of Dollar-Cost Averaging**: Reduces the risk of investing a large amount of money at an inopportune time, promotes disciplined investing.
- **Implementing Dollar-Cost Averaging**: Set up automatic investments into a diversified portfolio.

Workbook Activity: Dollar-Cost Averaging Plan

Create a dollar-cost averaging plan to systematically invest in your chosen assets.

Investment Type	Amount Per Interval	Interval (e.g., Monthly)	Start Date
Stocks			
Bonds			
Mutual Funds/ ETFs			
Real Estate			

5.3.2: Compound Interest and Long-Term Growth

Understanding and harnessing the power of compound interest is crucial for long-term wealth growth.

- **What Is Compound Interest?** The process of earning interest on both the initial principal and the accumulated interest from previous periods.
- **The Rule of 72**: A simple formula to estimate the number of years required to double an investment at a fixed annual rate of return.
- **Maximizing Compound Interest**: Start investing early, reinvest earnings, and maintain a long-term investment horizon.

Workbook Activity: Compound Interest Calculation

Calculate the potential growth of an investment using compound interest.

Initial Investment	Annual Interest Rate	Years	Future Value (Compound Interest)

5.3.3: Tax-Advantaged Accounts

Utilizing tax-advantaged accounts can enhance your investment returns by reducing your tax liability.

- **Types of Tax-Advantaged Accounts**: Individual Retirement Accounts (IRAs), 401(k) plans, Health Savings Accounts (HSAs), and 529 college savings plans.
- **Benefits of Tax-Advantaged Accounts**: Tax deferral, tax-free growth, and potential tax deductions.
- **Choosing the Right Account**: Consider your financial goals, tax situation, and investment horizon.

Workbook Activity: Tax-Advantaged Account Plan

Determine which tax-advantaged accounts are suitable for your financial goals and create a plan to utilize them effectively.

Account Type	Contribution Limit	Tax Benefits	Investment Options
IRA			
401(k)			
HSA			
529 Plan			

5.3.4: Diversifying Income Streams

Creating multiple income streams can enhance financial

security and accelerate wealth building.

- **Types of Income Streams**: Earned income, investment income, passive income, and business income.
- **Strategies for Diversifying Income**: Investing in real estate, dividend-paying stocks, side businesses, and freelance work.
- **Managing Multiple Income Streams**: Track income sources, allocate funds to investments, and adjust as needed.

Workbook Activity: Income Diversification Plan

Identify potential income streams and create a plan to develop and manage them.

Income Source	Type of Income	Potential Earnings	Actions Needed
Primary Job	Earned Income		
Real Estate	Passive Income		
Dividend Stocks	Investment Income		
Side Business	Business Income		

5.3.5: Financial Education and Continuous Learning

Ongoing financial education is essential for adapting to changing markets and improving investment decisions.

- **Importance of Financial Education**: Staying informed about market trends, investment strategies, and financial products.
- **Resources for Financial Learning**: Books, online courses, financial news, and professional advice.
- **Building a Financial Knowledge Base**: Regularly read financial literature, attend seminars, and engage with financial communities.

Workbook Activity: Financial Education Plan

Develop a plan to enhance your financial knowledge and stay informed about investment opportunities.

Learning Resource	Type (Book, Course, etc.)	Frequency of Use	Notes

Chapter Quiz

1. What are the main types of investments and their key characteristics?

    ◦ Answer: Stocks (ownership in a company, high returns and risk), bonds (debt securities, fixed interest payments, lower risk), mutual funds/ETFs (pooled investments, diversification), real estate (property investment, income and appreciation), alternative investments (commodities, hedge funds, high risk and fees).

2. How does diversification reduce investment risk?

    ◦ Answer: By spreading investments across various asset classes, industries, and geographies, diversification reduces the impact of any single investment's poor performance.

3. What is dollar-cost averaging, and what are its benefits?

    ◦ Answer: Dollar-cost averaging involves investing a fixed amount of money at regular intervals, reducing the risk of investing a large amount at an inopportune time and promoting disciplined investing.

4. How can tax-advantaged accounts enhance investment returns?

    ◦ Answer: Tax-advantaged accounts offer benefits such as tax deferral, tax-free growth, and potential tax deductions, reducing overall tax liability and enhancing investment returns.

5. Why is ongoing financial education important for

investors?

- Answer: Ongoing financial education helps investors stay informed about market trends, investment strategies, and financial products, enabling them to make better investment decisions and adapt to changing markets.

Chapter 5: Key Takeaways

1. **Understand Different Types of Investments**: Learn about stocks, bonds, mutual funds/ETFs, real estate, and alternative investments to build a diversified portfolio.

2. **Create a Diversified Investment Portfolio** Use asset allocation and diversification to manage risk and enhance potential returns.

3. **Implement Growth Strategies**: Utilize dollar-cost averaging, compound interest, tax-advantaged accounts, and income diversification to grow your wealth over time.

4. **Maintain Financial Education**: Continuously improve your financial knowledge to stay informed about investment opportunities and make better decisions.

5. **Monitor and Adjust Your Portfolio**: Regularly review and rebalance your portfolio to ensure it aligns with your financial goals and risk tolerance.

With a solid understanding of investment principles and strategies for building long-term wealth, it is time to focus on protecting and preserving your financial achievements. In Chapter 6, we will explore strategies for risk management, estate planning, and ensuring your financial legacy. By implementing these strategies, you can safeguard your wealth and ensure that your financial goals are achieved for generations to come.

CHAPTER 6:
PROTECTING AND
PRESERVING YOUR
FINANCIAL LEGACY

Building wealth is only one part of achieving financial stability and security. Protecting and preserving your financial legacy ensures that your hard-earned assets are safeguarded against unforeseen risks and can be passed on to future generations. This chapter will explore comprehensive strategies for risk management, estate planning, and legacy preservation. By implementing these strategies, you can ensure that your financial achievements are not only maintained but also continue to benefit your loved ones long after you are gone.

6.1: Risk Management Strategies

Effective risk management is crucial for protecting your financial assets against potential threats. This section will cover various types of risks and strategies to mitigate them, including insurance, diversification, and emergency planning.

6.1.1: Types of Financial Risks

Understanding the different types of financial risks is the first step in developing a robust risk management strategy.

- **Market Risk**: The risk of losses due to changes in market prices.
- **Credit Risk**: The risk of a borrower defaulting on a loan or debt.
- **Liquidity Risk**: The risk of being unable to sell an asset quickly without a significant loss.
- **Inflation Risk**: The risk that inflation will erode the purchasing power of your money.
- **Longevity Risk**: The risk of outliving your savings and financial resources.

6.1.2: Insurance as a Risk Management Tool

Insurance is a critical component of risk management, providing financial protection against various risks.

- **Types of Insurance**: Health insurance, life insurance, disability insurance, homeowners/renters insurance, auto insurance, and long-term care insurance.
- **Benefits of Insurance**: Provides financial protection, peace of mind, and ensures continuity of income and assets.
- **Choosing the Right Insurance Policies**: Assess your needs, compare policies, and ensure adequate coverage.

Workbook Activity: Insurance Needs Assessment

Evaluate your current insurance coverage and identify areas where additional protection may be needed.

Insurance Type	Current Coverage	Recommended Coverage	Notes
Health Insurance			
Life Insurance			
Disability Insurance			
Homeowners/Renters Insurance			
Auto Insurance			

Long-Term Care Insurance			

6.1.3: Diversification to Reduce Risk

Diversification is a strategy that spreads investment risk across various assets, reducing the impact of any single investment's poor performance.

- **Diversification Across Asset Classes**: Investing in a mix of stocks, bonds, real estate, and alternative investments.

- **Geographic Diversification**: Spreading investments across different countries and regions to reduce exposure to local market risks.

- **Sector Diversification**: Investing in various industries and sectors to mitigate sector-specific risks.

Workbook Activity: Diversification Plan

Create a diversification plan to spread your investment risk across different asset classes, geographies, and sectors.

Asset Class	Target Allocation (%)	Current Allocation (%)	Actions Needed
Stocks			
Bonds			
Real Estate			
Alternative Investments			
Geographic Diversification			
Sector Diversification			

6.1.4: Emergency Planning

An emergency plan ensures that you are prepared for unexpected financial shocks, such as job loss, medical emergencies, or natural disasters.

- **Building an Emergency Fund**: Save three to six months' worth of living expenses in a readily accessible account.

- **Creating a Contingency Plan**: Identify potential risks and outline steps to mitigate them.

- **Reviewing and Updating Your Plan**: Regularly review

and update your emergency plan to ensure it remains relevant.

Workbook Activity: Emergency Planning Checklist

Develop an emergency plan to prepare for unexpected financial shocks.

Emergency Planning Step	Description	Timeline
Build Emergency Fund	Save three to six months' worth of expenses	Ongoing
Identify Potential Risks	Assess possible financial shocks	Initial Planning
Create Contingency Plan	Outline steps to mitigate risks	Initial Planning
Review and Update Plan	Regularly review and update emergency plan	Annually/Semi-Annually

6.2: Estate Planning

Estate planning involves preparing for the management and distribution of your assets after your death. It ensures that your wishes are carried out, your loved ones are provided for, and potential estate taxes and legal issues are minimized.

6.2.1: Importance of Estate Planning

Proper estate planning provides peace of mind and ensures that your assets are distributed according to your wishes.

- **Benefits of Estate Planning**: Protects your assets, provides for your loved ones, minimizes estate taxes, and avoids probate delays.
- **Common Estate Planning Documents**: Wills, trusts, powers of attorney, and healthcare directives.
- **When to Start Estate Planning**: The earlier, the better;

review and update your plan regularly.

Workbook Activity: Estate Planning Basics

Assess your current estate planning needs and identify key documents to prepare.

Estate Planning Document	Description	Current Status
Will	Document outlining asset distribution	Not Started/In Progress/Complete
Trust	Legal arrangement to manage assets	Not Started/In Progress/Complete
Power of Attorney	Designates someone to make financial decisions	Not Started/In Progress/Complete
Healthcare Directive	Specifies medical treatment preferences	Not Started/In Progress/Complete

6.2.2: Creating a Will

A will is a legal document that outlines how your assets will be distributed after your death.

- **Components of a Will**: Executor, beneficiaries, asset distribution, and guardianship for minor children.
- **Drafting a Will**: Work with an attorney to ensure your will is legally valid and comprehensive.
- **Updating Your Will**: Regularly review and update your will to reflect changes in your life circumstances.

Workbook Activity: Will Preparation Checklist

Prepare a checklist to ensure all key components are included in your will.

Will Component	Description	Status
Executor	Person responsible for executing the will	Not Started/In Progress/Complete
Beneficiaries	Individuals who will receive assets	Not Started/In Progress/Complete
Asset Distribution	Specific instructions for asset distribution	Not Started/In Progress/Complete

Guardianship	Designation of guardians for minor children	Not Started/In Progress/Complete

6.2.3: Establishing Trusts

Trusts are legal arrangements that manage and protect assets on behalf of beneficiaries.

- **Types of Trusts**: Revocable trusts, irrevocable trusts, living trusts, testamentary trusts, and special needs trusts.

- **Benefits of Trusts**: Avoid probate, provide privacy, protect assets, and manage estate taxes.

- **Setting Up a Trust**: Work with an attorney to establish and fund the trust, ensuring it aligns with your estate planning goals.

Workbook Activity: Trust Planning Guide

Identify the types of trusts that may be beneficial for your estate plan and outline the steps to establish them.

Trust Type	Description	Benefits
Revocable Trust	Can be altered or revoked during the grantor's lifetime	Avoids probate, provides flexibility
Irrevocable Trust	Cannot be altered once established	Protects assets, reduces estate taxes
Living Trust	Established during the grantor's lifetime	Manages assets while alive and after death
Testamentary Trust	Created through a will after death	Provides for beneficiaries after death
Special Needs Trust	Supports individuals with disabilities	Preserves eligibility for government benefits

6.2.4: Powers of Attorney and Healthcare Directives

Powers of attorney and healthcare directives ensure that your financial and medical decisions are made according to your wishes if you become incapacitated.

- **Power of Attorney**: Designates someone to make

financial decisions on your behalf.

- **Healthcare Directive**: Specifies your preferences for medical treatment and designates a healthcare proxy.
- **Choosing the Right Individuals**: Select trustworthy and capable individuals to act on your behalf.

Workbook Activity: Powers of Attorney and Healthcare Directives

Prepare and document your powers of attorney and healthcare directives.

Document	Description	Designated Individual	Status
Power of Attorney	Financial decision-maker		Not Started/ In Progress/ Complete
Healthcare Directive	Medical treatment preferences		Not Started/ In Progress/ Complete
Healthcare Proxy	Person to make medical decisions		Not Started/ In Progress/ Complete

6.3: Legacy Preservation And Philanthropy

Preserving your financial legacy involves planning for the long-term management and distribution of your assets, including charitable giving. This section will explore strategies for legacy preservation and effective philanthropy.

6.3.1: Long-Term Financial Planning

Long-term financial planning ensures that your assets are managed and preserved for future generations.

- **Setting Long-Term Goals**: Define your legacy goals and create a plan to achieve them.
- **Family Involvement**: Communicate your plans with family members to ensure they understand and respect your wishes.
- **Professional Guidance**: Work with financial advisors, estate planners, and attorneys to implement your long-term plans.

Workbook Activity: Long-Term Financial Goals

Define your long-term financial goals and outline the steps to achieve them.

Goal	Description	Timeline	Actions Needed
Preserve Wealth	Ensure assets are managed and protected	Ongoing	Regular reviews and adjustments
Provide for Family	Plan for the financial security of family members	Ongoing	Communicate plans, update documents
Charitable Giving	Incorporate philanthropy into your legacy	Ongoing	Establish charitable trusts or foundations

6.3.2: Charitable Giving and Philanthropy

Incorporating charitable giving into your estate plan can create a lasting impact and reflect your values.

- **Benefits of Charitable Giving**: Provides tax benefits, supports causes you care about, and enhances your legacy.

- **Types of Charitable Giving**: Direct donations, donor-advised funds, charitable trusts, and private foundations.

- **Planning Your Charitable Giving**: Identify causes, choose giving methods, and integrate philanthropy into your estate plan.

Workbook Activity: Charitable Giving Plan

Develop a plan for incorporating charitable giving into your estate plan.

Charitable Cause	Type of Giving	Benefits	Timeline

6.3.3: Creating a Family Legacy Plan

A family legacy plan outlines how your values, traditions, and assets will be passed on to future generations.

- **Defining Your Legacy**: Identify the values, traditions, and goals you want to pass on.

- **Involving Family Members**: Engage family members in discussions about your legacy and involve them in planning.
- **Documenting Your Plan**: Create a comprehensive family legacy plan that includes financial and non-financial aspects.

Workbook Activity: Family Legacy Planning Guide

Create a family legacy plan to ensure your values and assets are preserved for future generations.

Legacy Component	Description	Actions Needed	Timeline
Values and Traditions	Define and document family values and traditions	Communicate with family	Ongoing
Financial Assets	Plan for the distribution and management of assets	Establish trusts, update wills	Ongoing
Charitable Involvement	Incorporate philanthropy into family legacy	Establish giving plans	Ongoing

Chapter Quiz

1. What are the main types of financial risks, and how can they be mitigated?

    - Answer: Market risk, credit risk, liquidity risk, inflation risk, and longevity risk can be mitigated through diversification, insurance, emergency planning, and careful financial management.

2. What are the benefits of creating a will, and what key components should it include?

    - Answer: A will ensures assets are distributed according to your wishes, protects loved ones, and minimizes legal complications. Key components include an executor, beneficiaries, asset distribution instructions, and guardianship designations.

3. How can trusts be used in estate planning, and what are some common types of trusts?

    - Answer: Trusts manage and protect assets, avoid probate, provide privacy, and reduce estate taxes. Common types include revocable trusts, irrevocable trusts, living trusts, testamentary trusts, and special needs trusts.

4. Why are powers of attorney and healthcare directives important in estate planning?

    - Answer: They ensure that financial and medical decisions are made according to your wishes if you become incapacitated. They designate trusted individuals to act on your behalf and specify your treatment preferences.

5. What strategies can be used for effective charitable

giving and preserving a family legacy?

- Answer: Strategies include direct donations, donor-advised funds, charitable trusts, and private foundations. Engaging family members, defining values and traditions, and creating a comprehensive family legacy plan are also important.

Chapter 6: Key Takeaways

1. **Understand and Manage Financial Risks**: Identify different types of financial risks and implement strategies such as insurance, diversification, and emergency planning to mitigate them.

2. **Develop a Comprehensive Estate Plan**: Create and regularly update key documents such as wills, trusts, powers of attorney, and healthcare directives to ensure your assets are managed and distributed according to your wishes.

3. **Incorporate Charitable Giving into Your Legacy**: Plan for charitable giving to support causes you care about, provide tax benefits, and enhance your legacy.

4. **Create a Family Legacy Plan**: Define and document your values, traditions, and goals to pass on to future generations, and involve family members in the planning process.

5. **Seek Professional Guidance**: Work with financial advisors, estate planners, and attorneys to implement and maintain your estate plan and legacy goals.

With a comprehensive understanding of risk management, estate planning, and legacy preservation, you are well equipped to protect your financial achievements. In Chapter 7, we will focus on continuous financial monitoring and adjustment to ensure your financial plan remains effective and aligned with your goals. We will explore strategies for regularly reviewing and adjusting your financial plan, staying informed about financial trends, and making proactive decisions to achieve long-term financial success.

CHAPTER 7: CONTINUOUS FINANCIAL MONITORING AND ADJUSTMENT

F inancial planning is not a one-time event but an ongoing process that requires regular monitoring and adjustment. With a strong foundation in place from the previous chapters—understanding your financial situation, building a solid financial foundation, managing debt, improving credit, investing wisely, and protecting your legacy—it's essential to ensure your financial plan remains aligned with your goals. In this chapter, we will explore strategies for continuous financial monitoring and adjustment, staying informed about financial trends, and making proactive decisions to achieve long-term financial success.

7.1: Regular Financial Check-Ups

Regular financial check-ups are crucial for maintaining financial health. This section will guide you through the process of conducting periodic reviews of your financial situation to ensure you stay on track.

7.1.1: Setting a Financial Review Schedule

Establishing a regular schedule for reviewing your financial situation helps you stay organized and proactive.

- **Monthly Reviews**: Monitor cash flow, track spending, and review budget.
- **Quarterly Reviews**: Assess investment performance, review savings goals, and adjust spending.
- **Annual Reviews**: Conduct a comprehensive review of your financial plan, including net worth, debt, investments, and insurance coverage.

Workbook Activity: Financial Review Schedule

Create a financial review schedule to ensure regular monitoring of your financial situation.

Review Frequency	Focus Areas	Notes
Monthly	Cash flow, spending, budget	
Quarterly	Investment performance, savings goals	
Annual	Comprehensive financial plan review	

7.1.2: Tracking Your Progress

Tracking your progress against your financial goals helps you stay motivated and make necessary adjustments.

- **Setting Benchmarks**: Establish clear benchmarks for each financial goal.
- **Using Financial Tools**: Leverage financial software and apps to track progress and generate reports.
- **Reviewing Progress**: Regularly compare your progress against your benchmarks and adjust your plan as needed.

Workbook Activity: Progress Tracking Template

Use this template to track your progress towards your financial goals.

Goal	Benchmark	Current Status	Actions Needed
Debt Reduction	% Debt Paid Off		
Savings	Amount Saved		
Investment Growth	% Portfolio Growth		

7.2: Staying Informed About Financial Trends

Staying informed about financial trends and market conditions is essential for making proactive decisions. This section will explore ways to keep up with financial news and insights.

7.2.1: Financial News and Resources

Accessing reliable financial news and resources helps you stay updated on market trends and economic developments.

- **Reputable News Sources**: Follow trusted financial news outlets such as Bloomberg, Reuters, and The Wall Street Journal.
- **Financial Websites and Blogs**: Read financial websites and blogs that offer expert analysis and insights.
- **Podcasts and Webinars**: Listen to financial podcasts and attend webinars to learn from industry experts.

Workbook Activity: Financial News Tracking

Identify and track reliable financial news sources to stay informed about market trends.

Source	Type (Website, Podcast, etc.)	Frequency of Use	Notes
Bloomberg	Website	Daily	
Reuters	Website	Daily	
The Wall Street Journal	Newspaper	Weekly	
Financial Podcasts	Podcast	Weekly	

7.2.2: Financial Education and Skill Building

Continuous learning and skill building are vital for making informed financial decisions.

- **Courses and Certifications**: Enroll in financial courses and obtain certifications to enhance your knowledge.
- **Books and Articles**: Read books and articles by financial experts to deepen your understanding.
- **Networking and Mentorship**: Connect with financial professionals and seek mentorship for personalized advice.

Workbook Activity: Financial Education Plan

Develop a plan to enhance your financial knowledge and skills.

Learning Resource	Type (Book, Course, etc.)	Frequency of Use	Notes
Financial Courses	Online Courses	Monthly	
Books by Financial Experts	Books	Monthly	
Financial Mentorship	Mentorship Sessions	Quarterly	

7.3: Making Proactive Financial Adjustments

Making proactive financial adjustments ensures that your financial plan remains relevant and effective in achieving your goals. This section will guide you through the process of adjusting your financial plan based on changing circumstances.

7.3.1: Adjusting Your Budget

Regularly reviewing and adjusting your budget helps you manage your finances effectively.

- **Identifying Changes in Income and Expenses**: Track any changes in your income and expenses and adjust your budget accordingly.
- **Reallocating Funds**: Reallocate funds to prioritize savings, debt repayment, and investments.
- **Setting New Financial Goals**: Update your financial goals based on your current financial situation.

Workbook Activity: Budget Adjustment Template

Use this template to adjust your budget based on changes in

your financial situation.

Income Source	Previous Amount	New Amount	Notes
Salary			
Freelance Work			
Investment Income			

Expense Category	Previous Amount	New Amount	Notes
Housing			
Utilities			
Food			

7.3.2: Rebalancing Your Investment Portfolio

Rebalancing your investment portfolio ensures that it remains aligned with your risk tolerance and financial goals.

- **When to Rebalance**: Rebalance your portfolio annually or when your asset allocation deviates significantly from your target.
- **How to Rebalance**: Sell over performing assets and buy underperforming ones to restore your target allocation.
- **Monitoring Market Conditions**: Stay informed about market conditions to make timely rebalancing decisions.

Workbook Activity: Portfolio Rebalancing Plan

Create a plan to rebalance your investment portfolio regularly.

Asset Class	Target Allocation (%)	Current Allocation (%)	Actions Needed
Stocks			
Bonds			
Real Estate			

7.3.3: Updating Insurance Coverage

Regularly reviewing and updating your insurance coverage ensures that you are adequately protected against potential risks.

- **Assessing Coverage Needs**: Evaluate your current insurance coverage and identify any gaps.
- **Adjusting Coverage**: Update your insurance policies to reflect changes in your financial situation and risk exposure.
- **Comparing Insurance Providers**: Shop around for the best insurance rates and coverage options.

Workbook Activity: Insurance Coverage Review

Review and update your insurance coverage to ensure adequate protection.

Insurance Type	Current Coverage	Recommended Coverage	Notes
Health Insurance			
Life Insurance			
Disability Insurance			

7.4: Seeking Professional Financial Advice

Professional financial advice can provide valuable insights and personalized strategies to enhance your financial plan. This section will explore how to find and work with financial advisors.

7.4.1: Finding the Right Financial Advisor

Choosing the right financial advisor is crucial for receiving effective and trustworthy advice.

- **Types of Financial Advisors**: Understand the different types of financial advisors, such as fee-only, commission-based, and fiduciary advisors.
- **Credentials and Experience**: Look for advisors with relevant credentials, such as Certified Financial Planner (CFP), and significant experience.
- **Interviewing Advisors**: Ask potential advisors about their approach, services, fees, and track record.

Workbook Activity: Financial Advisor Selection Checklist

Use this checklist to evaluate and select a suitable financial advisor.

Criteria	Notes	Advisor 1	Advisor 2
Credentials			
Experience			
Services Offered			
Fee Structure			
Client Reviews			

7.4.2: Working with Your Financial Advisor

Effectively working with your financial advisor ensures that you receive the maximum benefit from their expertise.

- **Setting Clear Goals**: Clearly communicate your financial goals and expectations.
- **Regular Communication**: Maintain regular communication with your advisor to review progress and make adjustments.
- **Reviewing Performance**: Regularly review the performance of your financial plan and make necessary changes based on your advisor's recommendations.

Workbook Activity: Financial Advisor Engagement Plan

Create a plan for engaging and working with your financial advisor.

Engagement Activity	Description	Frequency	Notes
Initial Consultation	Discuss goals, expectations, and services	One-time	
Regular Check-Ins	Review progress and adjust plan	Quarterly	
Performance Review	Assess plan performance and make changes	Annually	

Chapter Quiz

1. Why it is important to conduct regular financial check-ups and what should they include?
    - Answer: Regular financial check-ups help maintain financial health by monitoring cash flow, tracking spending, reviewing budgets, assessing investment performance, and ensuring adequate insurance coverage.

2. How can staying informed about financial trends benefit your financial plan?
    - Answer: Staying informed about financial trends helps you make proactive decisions, adapt to market conditions, and identify new opportunities for growth.

3. What are some key steps to take when making proactive financial adjustments?
    - Answer: Adjust your budget based on changes in income and expenses, rebalance your investment portfolio, and update your insurance coverage to reflect changes in your financial situation.

4. How can a financial advisor assist in enhancing your financial plan?
    - Answer: A financial advisor provides expert advice, personalized strategies, and ongoing support to help you achieve your financial goals and navigate complex financial decisions.

5. What should you consider when selecting a financial advisor?
    - Answer: Consider their credentials, experience, fee structure, services offered,

and client reviews to ensure they are qualified and a good fit for your needs.

Chapter 7: Key Takeaways

1. **Conduct Regular Financial Check-Ups**: Establish a schedule for reviewing your financial situation to stay on track with your goals.

2. **Track Your Progress**: Monitor your progress against benchmarks and adjust your plan as needed.

3. **Stay Informed About Financial Trends**: Keep up with reliable financial news and continuously enhance your financial knowledge and skills.

4. **Make Proactive Financial Adjustments**: Regularly adjust your budget, rebalance your investment portfolio, and update your insurance coverage.

5. **Seek Professional Financial Advice**: Work with a qualified financial advisor to receive personalized guidance and support in achieving your financial goals.

With a strong foundation in continuous financial monitoring and adjustment, you are well prepared to navigate your financial journey with confidence. In Chapter 8, we will explore advanced financial strategies for wealth accumulation and preservation. These strategies will help you optimize your financial plan, maximize your returns, and ensure long-term financial security for you and your family.

CHAPTER 8:
ADVANCED FINANCIAL
STRATEGIES
FOR WEALTH
ACCUMULATION AND
PRESERVATION

As you continue to build and protect your wealth, advanced financial strategies can help you optimize your financial plan, maximize your returns, and ensure long-term financial security. This chapter will delve into sophisticated techniques for wealth accumulation and preservation, including tax optimization, retirement planning, strategic philanthropy, and leveraging technology. By implementing these strategies, you can take your financial planning to the next level and secure a prosperous future for yourself and your family.

8.1: Tax Optimization Strategies

Tax optimization is a crucial aspect of advanced financial planning. By strategically managing your taxes, you can minimize your tax liability and maximize your after-tax income. This section will explore various tax optimization strategies, including tax-efficient investments, tax-advantaged accounts, and charitable giving.

8.1.1: Tax-Efficient Investments

Investing in tax-efficient vehicles can help reduce the amount of taxes you pay on your investment income.

- **Types of Tax-Efficient Investments**: Municipal bonds, index funds, ETFs, and tax-managed funds.

- **Benefits of Tax-Efficient Investments**: Lower capital gains taxes, tax-free interest income, and reduced taxable distributions.

- **Strategies for Tax-Efficient Investing**: Invest in tax-advantaged accounts, use tax-loss harvesting, and hold investments long-term to benefit from lower capital gains rates.

Workbook Activity: Tax-Efficient Investment Plan

Create a plan to incorporate tax-efficient investments into your portfolio.

Investment Type	Tax Benefits	Current Allocation (%)	Target Allocation (%)
Municipal Bonds	Tax-free interest		
Index Funds	Lower capital gains		
ETFs	Reduced taxable distributions		
Tax-Managed Funds	Tax-efficient strategies		

8.1.2: Utilizing Tax-Advantaged Accounts

Tax-advantaged accounts can significantly enhance your tax savings and boost your retirement savings.

- **Types of Tax-Advantaged Accounts**: Traditional IRAs, Roth IRAs, 401(k) plans, Health Savings Accounts (HSAs), and 529 college savings plans.

- **Benefits of Tax-Advantaged Accounts**: Tax deductions, tax-deferred growth, and tax-free withdrawals.
- **Maximizing Contributions**: Contribute the maximum allowable amounts to your tax-advantaged accounts each year.

Workbook Activity: Tax-Advantaged Account Contribution Plan

Plan your contributions to tax-advantaged accounts to maximize your tax savings.

Account Type	Contribution Limit	Current Contribution	Target Contribution
Traditional IRA			
Roth IRA			
401(k)			
HSA			
529 Plan			

8.1.3: Strategic Charitable Giving

Incorporating charitable giving into your financial plan can provide tax benefits while supporting causes you care about.

- **Benefits of Charitable Giving**: Tax deductions, reduced taxable income, and potential estate tax benefits.
- **Types of Charitable Giving**: Direct donations, donor-advised funds, charitable remainder trusts, and private foundations.
- **Planning Your Charitable Giving**: Identify causes, choose giving methods, and integrate philanthropy into your estate plan.

Workbook Activity: Charitable Giving Strategy

Develop a strategic plan for charitable giving to optimize tax benefits and support your chosen causes.

Charitable Cause	Type of Giving	Tax Benefits	Annual Contribution

8.2: Advanced Retirement Planning

Advanced retirement planning involves creating a comprehensive strategy to ensure you can maintain your desired lifestyle in retirement. This section will cover retirement income strategies, Social Security optimization, and healthcare planning.

8.2.1: Retirement Income Strategies

Developing a diversified income plan is essential for a secure and comfortable retirement.

- **Sources of Retirement Income**: Social Security, pensions, retirement accounts, annuities, and investment income.
- **Creating a Withdrawal Strategy**: Determine the optimal withdrawal rate to ensure your retirement savings last throughout your retirement.
- **Balancing Risk and Return**: Adjust your investment portfolio to balance growth potential with risk management in retirement.

Workbook Activity: Retirement Income Plan

Create a comprehensive plan for generating income in retirement.

Income Source	Estimated Amount	Withdrawal Strategy	Notes
Social Security			
Pensions			
Retirement Accounts			
Annuities			
Investment Income			

8.2.2: Social Security Optimization

Maximizing your Social Security benefits is a key component of retirement planning.

- **Understanding Social Security Benefits**: Learn how your benefits are calculated and the factors that affect them.

- **Optimal Claiming Strategies**: Determine the best age to start claiming benefits based on your personal circumstances.
- **Spousal and Survivor Benefits**: Explore strategies for maximizing spousal and survivor benefits.

Workbook Activity: Social Security Optimization Plan

Develop a plan to optimize your Social Security benefits.

Strategy	Description	Estimated Benefit Increase	Notes
Claiming Age	Determine optimal age to claim benefits		
Spousal Benefits	Explore spousal benefit options		
Survivor Benefits	Plan for maximizing survivor benefits		

8.2.3: Healthcare and Long-Term Care Planning

Healthcare and long-term care expenses can be significant in retirement, making it essential to plan for these costs.

- **Health Insurance Options**: Understand your health insurance options, including Medicare, Medigap, and Medicare Advantage plans.
- **Long-Term Care Insurance**: Evaluate the benefits and costs of long-term care insurance to cover potential long-term care needs.
- **Healthcare Savings Strategies**: Utilize Health Savings Accounts (HSAs) and other savings strategies to prepare for healthcare expenses.

Workbook Activity: Healthcare and Long-Term Care Plan

Create a plan to manage healthcare and long-term care expenses in retirement.

ROBERTKNIGHT

Expense Category	Estimated Annual Cost	Funding Strategy	Notes
Health Insurance			
Out-of-Pocket Expenses			
Long-Term Care			

8.3: Strategic Philanthropy And Legacy Planning

Strategic philanthropy and legacy planning allow you to make a lasting impact while preserving your wealth for future generations. This section will cover advanced strategies for charitable giving, legacy planning, and family governance.

8.3.1: Creating a Charitable Legacy

Incorporating philanthropy into your legacy plan can create a lasting impact and reflect your values.

- **Types of Charitable Structures**: Donor-advised funds, charitable remainder trusts, private foundations, and charitable lead trusts.
- **Benefits of Charitable Giving**: Tax benefits, support for causes you care about, and enhanced family legacy.
- **Planning Your Charitable Legacy**: Define your philanthropic goals, choose the appropriate charitable structure, and integrate philanthropy into your estate plan.

Workbook Activity: Charitable Legacy Plan

Develop a plan to incorporate charitable giving into your legacy.

Charitable Structure	Description	Tax Benefits	Annual Contribution
Donor-Advised Fund			
Charitable Remainder Trust			
Private Foundation			
Charitable Lead Trust			

8.3.2: Advanced Legacy Planning Strategies

Advanced legacy planning ensures that your wealth is preserved and transferred according to your wishes.

- **Trust Structures**: Use complex trust structures to manage and protect assets, such as dynasty trusts, generation-skipping trusts, and asset protection trusts.
- **Family Limited Partnerships (FLPs)**: Establish FLPs to manage family assets, provide tax benefits, and facilitate generational wealth transfer.
- **Estate Tax Planning**: Implement strategies to minimize estate taxes, such as gifting, irrevocable life insurance trusts (ILITs), and charitable bequests.

Workbook Activity: Advanced Legacy Planning Guide

Identify and implement advanced strategies for preserving and transferring your wealth.

Strategy	Description	Benefits	Actions Needed
Dynasty Trust	Long-term asset management	Protects and grows wealth	Establish trust, fund it
Generation-Skipping Trust	Skips a generation for tax benefits	Reduces estate taxes	Establish trust, fund it
Family Limited Partnership	Manages family assets	Provides tax benefits	Establish partnership
Gifting Strategy	Transfers wealth during lifetime	Reduces estate taxes	Identify assets to gift

8.3.3: Family Governance and Communication

Establishing family governance structures and open communication can ensure that your legacy is preserved and respected.

- **Family Meetings and Councils**: Hold regular family meetings to discuss financial matters, educate family members, and make joint decisions.
- **Developing a Family Mission Statement**: Create a family mission statement to define your family's values, goals, and vision.
- **Educating Heirs**: Provide financial education and mentoring to prepare heirs for managing and

preserving family wealth.

Workbook Activity: Family Governance Plan

Create a plan for establishing family governance structures and promoting open communication.

Governance Activity	Description	Frequency	Notes
Family Meetings	Regular meetings to discuss financial matters	Quarterly	
Family Mission Statement	Define family values, goals, and vision	One-time, update as needed	
Their Education Program	Financial education and mentoring	Ongoing	

8.4: Leveraging Technology For Financial Management

Technology can enhance your financial management by providing tools for budgeting, investing, and tracking your financial progress. This section will explore various financial technologies and how to leverage them effectively.

8.4.1: Financial Planning Software

Using financial planning software can help you create and manage a comprehensive financial plan.

- **Types of Financial Planning Software**: Personal finance apps, robo-advisors, and comprehensive financial planning platforms.
- **Benefits of Financial Planning Software**: Automated budgeting, investment management, goal tracking, and financial insights.
- **Choosing the Right Software**: Evaluate different software options based on your needs, preferences, and budget.

Workbook Activity: Financial Planning Software Evaluation

Compare different financial planning software options to find the best fit for your needs.

Software Name	Features	Cost	Notes
Personal Finance App	Budgeting, expense tracking		
Robo-Advisor	Automated investment management		
Comprehensive Platform	Full financial planning, goal tracking		

8.4.2: Investment Platforms and Tools

Investment platforms and tools can streamline your investment process and provide valuable insights.

- **Online Brokerages**: Use online brokerage platforms for trading stocks, bonds, ETFs, and mutual funds.
- **Investment Research Tools**: Access research tools and resources to analyze investments and make informed decisions.
- **Automated Investing**: Leverage robo-advisors and automated investing platforms to manage your portfolio.

Workbook Activity: Investment Platform Comparison

Evaluate different investment platforms and tools to optimize your investment process.

Platform Name	Features	Cost	Notes
Online Brokerage	Trading, research tools		
Robo-Advisor	Automated portfolio management		
Research Tools	Investment analysis, market insights		

8.4.3: Budgeting and Expense Tracking Apps

Budgeting and expense tracking apps can help you manage your finances efficiently and stay on top of your spending.

- **Features of Budgeting Apps**: Expense tracking, budget creation, bill reminders, and financial goal setting.
- **Popular Budgeting Apps**: Mint, YNAB (You Need a

Budget), PocketGuard, and Personal Capital.

- **Integrating Apps with Your Financial Plan**: Use budgeting apps to complement your overall financial plan and track progress towards your goals.

Workbook Activity: Budgeting App Evaluation

Compare different budgeting apps to find the best fit for your financial management needs.

App Name	Features	Cost	Notes
Mint	Expense tracking, budget creation		
YNAB	Zero-based budgeting		
PocketGuard	Budget tracking, bill reminders		
Personal Capital	Budgeting, investment tracking		

Chapter Quiz

1. What are some tax optimization strategies for enhancing your financial plan?
   - Answer: Tax-efficient investments, utilizing tax-advantaged accounts, and strategic charitable giving.

2. How can you create a diversified retirement income plan?
   - Answer: Utilize various income sources such as Social Security, pensions, retirement accounts, annuities, and investment income, and develop a withdrawal strategy that balances risk and return.

3. What are some advanced legacy planning strategies for preserving and transferring wealth?
   - Answer: Use complex trust structures, establish Family Limited Partnerships (FLPs), implement estate tax planning strategies, and create a charitable legacy.

4. How can technology enhance your financial management?
   - Answer: Use financial planning software for comprehensive planning, investment platforms and tools for streamlined investing, and budgeting apps for efficient expense tracking and budget management.

5. What is the importance of family governance in legacy planning?
   - Answer: Family governance structures and open communication ensure that your legacy is preserved and respected, involving family members in financial decisions, defining

family values, and educating heirs.

Chapter 8: Key Takeaways

1. **Implement Tax Optimization Strategies**: Enhance your financial plan by incorporating tax-efficient investments, utilizing tax-advantaged accounts, and engaging in strategic charitable giving.

2. **Develop Advanced Retirement Plans**: Create a diversified retirement income plan, optimize Social Security benefits, and plan for healthcare and long-term care expenses.

3. **Incorporate Strategic Philanthropy and Legacy Planning**: Use advanced legacy-planning strategies, establish family governance structures, and create a charitable legacy to preserve and transfer wealth.

4. **Leverage Technology for Financial Management**: Utilize financial planning software, investment platforms, and budgeting apps to enhance your financial management and track your progress.

5. **Seek Professional Guidance**: Work with financial advisors and estate planners to implement advanced strategies and ensure your financial plan remains effective and aligned with your goals.

With advanced financial strategies in place, you are well equipped to optimize your financial plan and secure your long-term financial future. In Chapter 9, we will explore strategies for navigating major life events and transitions, such as career changes, marriage, parenthood, and retirement. By understanding and preparing for these events, you can make informed decisions and maintain financial stability throughout life's various stages.

CHAPTER 9: NAVIGATING MAJOR LIFE EVENTS AND TRANSITIONS

L ife is full of major events and transitions that can significantly affect your financial situation. From career changes and marriage to parenthood and retirement, each stage of life presents unique challenges and opportunities. This chapter will provide comprehensive strategies for navigating these key life events, ensuring that you are prepared to make informed decisions and maintain financial stability. By understanding and planning for these transitions, you can achieve your financial goals and secure a prosperous future.

9.1: Career Changes And Advancements

Career changes and advancements can have a significant impact on your financial situation. Whether you are transitioning to a new job, pursuing a promotion, or starting your own business, it is essential to manage these changes effectively.

9.1.1: Preparing for a Job Transition

Changing jobs can be both exciting and challenging. Proper preparation is key to ensuring a smooth transition.

- **Assessing Your Current Situation**: Evaluate your current job satisfaction, career goals, and financial needs.
- **Updating Your Resume and Skills**: Ensure your resume is up-to-date and reflect any new skills or accomplishments.
- **Researching Potential Employers**: Research potential employers to find a good match for your career goals and values.
- **Negotiating Salary and Benefits**: Be prepared to negotiate your salary and benefits to ensure you receive fair compensation.

Workbook Activity: Job Transition Plan

Create a plan to prepare for a job transition, including key steps and timelines.

Task	Description	Deadline	Notes
Assess Current Situation	Evaluate job satisfaction and career goals		
Update Resume	Revise resume and reflect new skills		
Research Employers	Identify potential employers and roles		
Negotiate Salary	Prepare for salary and benefits negotiation		

9.1.2: Pursuing Career Advancement

Advancing in your career can lead to increased income and job satisfaction. This subsection will explore strategies for achieving career growth.

- **Setting Career Goals**: Define your long-term career goals and create a plan to achieve them.
- **Developing New Skills**: Continuously improve your skills through education, training, and professional development.
- **Networking and Mentorship**: Build a strong professional network and seek mentorship to gain insights and guidance.
- **Seeking Opportunities for Growth**: Look for opportunities within your organization or industry to advance your career.

Workbook Activity: Career Advancement Plan

Develop a plan to achieve your career goals and pursue advancement opportunities.

Goal	Description	Actions Needed	Timeline
Long-Term Career Goal	Define long-term career aspirations		
Skill Development	Identify and pursue new skills		
Networking	Build professional network		
Growth Opportunities	Seek and evaluate growth opportunities		

9.1.3: Starting Your Own Business

Starting your own business can be a rewarding but challenging endeavor. Proper planning and preparation are essential for success.

- **Evaluating Business Ideas**: Assess the viability of your business idea and conduct market research.
- **Creating a Business Plan**: Develop a detailed business plan outlining your business goals, strategies, and financial projections.
- **Securing Funding**: Explore funding options such as personal savings, loans, investors, or crowdfunding.

- **Managing Business Finances**: Set up a system for managing your business finances, including budgeting, accounting, and tax planning.

Workbook Activity: Business Start-Up Plan

Create a comprehensive plan for starting your own business, including key steps and timelines.

Task	Description	Deadline	Notes
Evaluate Business Idea	Assess viability and conduct market research		
Create Business Plan	Develop detailed business plan		
Secure Funding	Explore funding options		
Manage Finances	Set up financial management system		

9.2: Marriage And Financial Planning

Marriage is a significant life event that brings together two individuals' financial lives. Effective financial planning is crucial for ensuring a successful and harmonious marriage.

9.2.1: Combining Finances

Combining finances can be a complex process. This subsection will explore strategies for merging financial accounts and managing joint expenses.

- **Discussing Financial Goals and Values**: Have open and honest discussions about your financial goals, values, and priorities.

- **Deciding on Joint or Separate Accounts**: Determine whether to combine all accounts, keep separate accounts, or use a combination of both.

- **Creating a Joint Budget**: Develop a budget that accounts for both partners' incomes, expenses, and savings goals.

- **Managing Joint Expenses**: Establish a system for

managing joint expenses, such as splitting costs or using a joint account.

Workbook Activity: Financial Plan for Marriage

Create a plan for combining finances and managing joint expenses.

Task	Description	Deadline	Notes
Discuss Financial Goals	Have open discussions about goals and values		
Decide on Accounts	Determine joint or separate accounts		
Create Joint Budget	Develop a budget for combined finances		
Manage Expenses	Establish system for managing expenses		

9.2.2: Planning for Major Purchases

Marriage often involves planning for major purchases such as a home, car, or vacations. Proper financial planning is essential for making these purchases without compromising your financial stability.

- **Setting Savings Goals**: Define savings goals for major purchases and create a plan to achieve them.
- **Creating a Savings Plan**: Develop a detailed savings plan, including timelines and monthly savings targets.
- **Evaluating Financing Options**: Research and compare financing options for major purchases, such as mortgages or auto loans.
- **Making Informed Decisions**: Make informed decisions based on your financial situation, goals, and available

financing options.

Workbook Activity: Major Purchase Plan

Develop a plan for saving and financing major purchases.

Purchase	Estimated Cost	Savings Goal	Financing Options
Home			
Car			
Vacation			

9.2.3: Protecting Your Assets

Protecting your assets is crucial for ensuring financial stability and security in marriage. This subsection will explore strategies for safeguarding your assets.

- **Insurance Coverage**: Ensure adequate insurance coverage for health, life, property, and liability.
- **Estate Planning**: Create or update wills, trusts, and other estate planning documents to reflect your marital status.
- **Legal Agreements**: Consider legal agreements such as prenuptial or postnuptial agreements to protect individual assets.
- **Financial Transparency**: Maintain open communication and transparency about financial matters to avoid misunderstandings.

Workbook Activity: Asset Protection Plan

Create a plan to protect your assets and ensure financial security.

Task	Description	Deadline	Notes
Review Insurance	Ensure adequate coverage		
Update Estate Plan	Create or update wills and trusts		
Consider Legal Agreements	Evaluate need for prenuptial/ postnuptial agreements		
Maintain Transparency	Communicate openly about		

9.3: Parenthood And Financial Planning

Parenthood brings new financial responsibilities and challenges. Proper financial planning is essential for providing for your children and ensuring their future security.

9.3.1: Preparing for Childbirth

Preparing for childbirth involves planning for both immediate and long-term financial needs.

- **Budgeting for Medical Expenses**: Estimate and plan for medical expenses related to childbirth and prenatal care.
- **Creating a Baby Budget**: Develop a budget for baby-related expenses, such as nursery setup, clothing, and supplies.
- **Reviewing Insurance Coverage**: Ensure your health insurance covers childbirth and pediatric care.
- **Building an Emergency Fund**: Increase your emergency fund to cover unexpected expenses related to childbirth.

Workbook Activity: Childbirth Preparation Plan

Create a plan to prepare for the financial aspects of childbirth.

Task	Description	Deadline	Notes
Budget for Medical Expenses	Estimate and plan for medical costs		
Create Baby Budget	Develop budget for baby-related expenses		
Review Insurance	Ensure coverage for childbirth and pediatric care		
Build Emergency Fund	Increase		

	emergency fund for unexpected expenses		

9.3.2: Saving for Education

Saving for your children's education is a significant financial goal. This subsection will explore strategies for funding education expenses.

- **Education Savings Accounts**: Utilize education savings accounts such as 529 plans and Coverdell ESAs.
- **Scholarships and Grants**: Research and apply for scholarships and grants to help offset education costs.
- **Setting Savings Goals**: Define savings goals for education expenses and create a plan to achieve them.
- **Exploring Financing Options**: Consider financing options such as student loans and work-study programs.

Workbook Activity: Education Savings Plan

Develop a plan to save for your children's education expenses.

Savings Account	Contribution Limit	Current Contribution	Target Contribution
529 Plan			
Coverdell ESA			

Scholarship/Grant	Application Deadline	Eligibility Criteria	Notes

9.3.3: Planning for Childcare and Activities

Childcare and extracurricular activities can be significant expenses. Proper planning is essential for managing these costs.

- **Budgeting for Childcare**: Estimate and plan for childcare expenses, including daycare, babysitting, and after-school programs.
- **Evaluating Childcare Options**: Research and compare different childcare options to find the best fit for your family.

- **Planning for Extracurricular Activities**: Budget for extracurricular activities such as sports, music lessons, and camps.
- **Maximizing Tax Benefits**: Utilize tax benefits such as the Child and Dependent Care Credit to offset childcare costs.

Workbook Activity: Childcare and Activity Plan

Create a plan to manage childcare and extracurricular activity expenses.

Childcare Option	Estimated Cost	Notes
Daycare		
Babysitting		
After-School Program		

Activity	Estimated Cost	Notes
Sports		
Music Lessons		
Camps		

9.4: Planning For Major Life Events

Life is full of significant events that require careful financial planning. This section will cover strategies for planning for major life events such as buying a home, planning vacations, and managing unexpected expenses.

9.4.1: Buying a Home

Buying a home is one of the most significant financial decisions you will make. Proper planning is essential to ensure you make an informed and financially sound purchase.

- **Assessing Your Financial Situation**: Evaluate your financial situation, including income, savings, and debt, to determine how much you can afford to spend on a home.
- **Saving for a Down Payment**: Create a savings plan to

accumulate the necessary funds for a down payment.

- **Researching Mortgages**: Compare different mortgage options to find the best fit for your financial situation.
- **Budgeting for Homeownership**: Develop a budget that accounts for all homeownership expenses, including mortgage payments, property taxes, insurance, and maintenance.

.

Workbook Activity: Home-Buying Plan

Create a comprehensive plan for buying a home, including key steps and timelines.

Task	Description	Deadline	Notes
Assess Financial Situation	Evaluate income, savings, and debt		
Save for Down Payment	Create savings plan		
Research Mortgages	Compare mortgage options		
Budget for Homeowne rship	Develop budget for home expenses		

9.4.2: Planning Vacations

Vacations are an essential part of maintaining work-life balance and overall well-being. Proper financial planning ensures you can enjoy your vacations without compromising your financial stability.

- **Setting a Vacation Budget**: Determine how much you can afford to spend on vacations and create a budget.
- **Saving for Vacations**: Develop a savings plan to accumulate the necessary funds for your vacations.
- **Finding Travel Deals**: Research and take advantage of travel deals, discounts, and rewards programs.

- **Planning Activities and Expenses**: Plan your vacation activities and estimate related expenses to stay within your budget.

Workbook Activity: Vacation Planning Guide

Create a plan to save for and manage vacation expenses.

Task	Description	Deadline	Notes
Set Vacation Budget	Determine affordable spending amount		
Save for Vacation	Develop savings plan		
Research Travel Deals	Find discounts and rewards programs		
Plan Activities	Estimate costs of vacation activities		

9.4.3: Managing Unexpected Expenses

Unexpected expenses can disrupt your financial plans. Having a strategy for managing these expenses is crucial for maintaining financial stability.

- **Building an Emergency Fund**: Ensure you have an emergency fund to cover unexpected expenses.
- **Insurance Coverage**: Maintain adequate insurance coverage to protect against unforeseen events.
- **Accessing Credit**: Have access to credit options, such as credit cards or lines of credit, for emergencies.
- **Adjusting Your Budget**: Be prepared to adjust your budget to accommodate unexpected expenses.

Workbook Activity: Unexpected Expense Plan

Create a plan to manage unexpected expenses and maintain financial stability.

Task	Description	Deadline	Notes
Build Emergency	Ensure		

Fund	sufficient funds for emergencies		
Review Insurance	Maintain adequate coverage		
Access Credit	Have credit options available		
Adjust Budget	Be prepared to adjust budget as needed		

9.5: Retirement Planning

Retirement planning is a lifelong process that requires careful planning and regular review. This section will cover strategies for building a retirement nest egg, managing retirement income, and ensuring a comfortable and secure retirement.

9.5.1: Building a Retirement Nest Egg

Accumulating sufficient savings for retirement is essential for maintaining your desired lifestyle in retirement.

- **Setting Retirement Goals**: Define your retirement goals and estimate the amount of savings needed to achieve them.
- **Creating a Savings Plan**: Develop a detailed savings plan, including contribution amounts and investment strategies.
- **Maximizing Retirement Accounts**: Take advantage of retirement accounts such as 401(k) plans, IRAs, and Roth IRAs.
- **Diversifying Investments**: Diversify your investments to balance risk and growth potential.

Workbook Activity: Retirement Savings Plan

Create a comprehensive plan for building your retirement nest egg.

Goal	Description	Savings Target	Actions Needed
Retirement Lifestyle	Define desired retirement lifestyle		
Estimate Savings Needed	Calculate required savings amount		
Create Savings Plan	Develop detailed savings plan		
Maximize Retirement Accounts	Contribute to retirement accounts		
Diversify Investments	Balance risk and growth potential		

9.5.2: Managing Retirement Income

Managing your income in retirement ensures that your savings last and you can maintain your desired lifestyle.

- **Creating a Withdrawal Strategy**: Develop a withdrawal strategy that balances income needs with the longevity of your savings.
- **Managing Investments in Retirement**: Adjust your investment portfolio to balance risk and income needs in retirement.
- **Exploring Income Sources**: Consider various income sources, such as Social Security, pensions, annuities, and part-time work.
- **Budgeting for Retirement**: Develop a retirement budget that accounts for all expenses and income sources.

Workbook Activity: Retirement Income Plan

Create a comprehensive plan for managing your retirement income.

Income Source	Estimated Amount	Withdrawal Strategy	Notes
Social Security			
Pensions			
Retirement Accounts			
Annuities			
Part-Time Work			

9.5.3: Ensuring Financial Security in Retirement

Ensuring financial security in retirement involves planning for healthcare, long-term care, and potential risks.

- **Planning for Healthcare Costs**: Estimate healthcare costs in retirement and plan for them.

- **Long-Term Care Planning**: Consider long-term care insurance and other strategies for managing long-term care costs.

- **Managing Financial Risks**: Mitigate financial risks through diversification, insurance, and contingency planning.

Workbook Activity: Retirement Security Plan

Create a plan to ensure financial security in retirement.

Task	Description	Deadline	Notes
Plan for Healthcare Costs	Estimate and plan for healthcare expenses		
Consider Long-Term Care	Evaluate long-term care insurance		
Manage Financial Risks	Diversify investments, maintain insurance		

Chapter Quiz

1. What are some key considerations when preparing for a job transition?

   ◦ Answer: Assessing your current situation, updating your resume and skills, researching potential employers, and negotiating salary and benefits.

2. How can couples effectively combine their finances and manage joint expenses?

   ◦ Answer: Discuss financial goals and values, decide on joint or separate accounts, create a joint budget, and establish a system for managing joint expenses.

3. What strategies can parents use to save for their children's education?

   ◦ Answer: Utilize education savings accounts such as 529 plans and Coverdell ESAs, research and apply for scholarships and grants, set savings goals, and explore financing options.

4. How can you plan for major purchases such as buying a home or planning vacations?

   ◦ Answer: Assess your financial situation, create a savings plan, research-financing options, and develop a budget for related expenses.

5. What steps can you take to ensure financial security in retirement?

   ◦ Answer: Set retirement goals, create a savings plan, maximize retirement accounts, diversify investments, develop a withdrawal strategy, manage investments in retirement, and plan for healthcare and long-term care costs.

Chapter 9: Key Takeaways

1. **Prepare for Career Changes and Advancements**: Properly plan for job transitions, pursue career growth opportunities, and consider starting your own business.

2. **Combine Finances and Plan for Marriage**: Discuss financial goals, create joint budgets, plan for major purchases, and protect your assets in marriage.

3. **Plan for Parenthood and Children's Future**: Prepare for childbirth expenses, save for education, and manage childcare and extracurricular activity costs.

4. **Plan for Major Life Events**: Create comprehensive plans for buying a home, planning vacations, and managing unexpected expenses.

5. **Ensure a Secure Retirement**: Build a retirement nest egg, manage retirement income, and ensure financial security through proper planning.

Having navigated the major life events and transitions with comprehensive financial strategies, you are now well prepared to continue your journey toward long-term financial success. In Chapter 10, we will explore the importance of financial resilience and adaptability, focusing on strategies to stay financially strong and agile in the face of economic changes, personal challenges, and unexpected opportunities. By building financial resilience, you can maintain stability and achieve your financial goals regardless of the circumstances.

CHAPTER 10: BUILDING FINANCIAL RESILIENCE AND ADAPTABILITY

I n an ever-changing world, financial resilience and adaptability are crucial for maintaining stability and achieving long-term financial goals. Life is full of uncertainties, from economic downturns and job losses to unexpected expenses and personal challenges. This chapter will provide comprehensive strategies for building financial resilience and adaptability, ensuring that you can navigate these uncertainties with confidence. By developing a strong financial foundation, creating emergency plans, and staying flexible in your financial planning, you can maintain stability and achieve your financial goals regardless of the circumstances.

10.1: Understanding Financial Resilience

Financial resilience is the ability to withstand and recover from financial shocks. It involves having the resources, skills, and strategies to manage unexpected financial challenges effectively.

10.1.1: Key Components of Financial Resilience

Understanding the key components of financial resilience can help you build a robust financial foundation.

- **Emergency Savings**: Having a sufficient emergency fund to cover unexpected expenses.
- **Diversified Income Sources**: Creating multiple streams of income to reduce reliance on a single source.
- **Adequate Insurance Coverage**: Ensuring you have the necessary insurance to protect against financial risks.
- **Financial Literacy**: Continuously improving your financial knowledge and skills to make informed decisions.

Workbook Activity: Financial Resilience Assessment

Evaluate your current financial resilience by assessing key components.

Component	Current Status	Actions Needed	Timeline
Emergency Savings			
Diversified Income			
Insurance Coverage			
Financial Literacy			

10.1.2: The Importance of Financial Resilience

Financial resilience is essential for maintaining stability and achieving long-term financial goals.

- **Coping with Financial Shocks**: Ability to manage unexpected expenses, job losses, and economic downturns.
- **Reducing Financial Stress**: Peace of mind knowing you have a plan to handle financial challenges.
- **Enhancing Financial Flexibility**: Ability to adapt to changing circumstances and seize opportunities.

Workbook Activity: Financial Resilience Goals

Define your financial resilience goals and create a plan to achieve them.

Goal	Description	Actions Needed	Timeline
Build Emergency Fund	Save three to six months' worth of expenses		
Diversify Income	Create additional income streams		
Review Insurance	Ensure adequate coverage		
Improve Financial Literacy	Take courses, read books, and attend seminars		

10.2: Building An Emergency Fund

An emergency fund is a cornerstone of financial resilience. It provides a financial buffer to cover unexpected expenses and helps you avoid going into debt during emergencies.

10.2.1: Determining the Size of Your Emergency Fund

The size of your emergency fund depends on your individual circumstances, including your income, expenses, and financial obligations.

- **Assessing Your Monthly Expenses**: Calculate your essential monthly expenses, including housing, utilities, food, transportation, and insurance.
- **Setting a Savings Goal**: Aim to save three to six months' worth of essential expenses in your emergency fund.
- **Adjusting for Personal Factors**: Consider factors such as job stability, health, and dependents when determining the size of your emergency fund.

Workbook Activity: Emergency Fund Calculation

Calculate the amount needed for your emergency fund based on your monthly expenses and personal factors.

Expense Category	Monthly Amount	Notes
Housing		
Utilities		
Food		
Transportation		
Insurance		
Other Essential Expenses		

10.2.2: Strategies for Building Your Emergency Fund

Building an emergency fund requires discipline and a structured savings plan.

- **Setting Up a Dedicated Savings Account**: Open a separate savings account specifically for your emergency fund.
- **Automating Savings**: Set up automatic transfers from your checking account to your emergency fund.
- **Reducing Expenses**: Identify areas where you can cut back on non-essential spending to boost your savings.
- **Increasing Income**: Consider side hustles or part-time work to accelerate your savings.

Workbook Activity: Emergency Fund Savings Plan

Create a plan to build your emergency fund, including specific actions and timelines.

Task	Description	Deadline	Notes
Open Savings Account	Set up a dedicated emergency fund account		
Automate Savings	Schedule automatic transfers		
Reduce Expenses	Identify and cut non-essential spending		

Increase Income	Explore side hustles or part-time work		

10.2.3: Maintaining Your Emergency Fund

Once you have built your emergency fund, it is important to maintain and replenish it as needed.

- **Using Your Emergency Fund Wisely**: Only use your emergency fund for genuine emergencies, not for discretionary spending.
- **Replenishing After Use**: If you need to use your emergency fund, prioritize replenishing it as soon as possible.
- **Regularly Reviewing Your Fund**: Periodically review the size of your emergency fund to ensure it still meets your needs.

Workbook Activity: Emergency Fund Maintenance Plan

Create a plan for maintaining and replenishing your emergency fund.

Task	Description	Frequency	Notes
Review Fund Size	Assess if the fund meets current needs	Annually	
Replenish Fund	Prioritize savings after using the fund	As needed	
Use Fund Wisely	Ensure fund is used only for emergencies	Ongoing	

10.3: Diversifying Income Sources

Having multiple income streams enhances financial resilience by reducing reliance on a single source of income and providing additional financial security.

10.3.1: Identifying Additional Income Streams

Explore various ways to diversify your income and identify opportunities that align with your skills and interests.

- **Freelancing and Consulting**: Offer your expertise and services on a freelance or consulting basis.
- **Part-Time or Seasonal Work**: Consider part-time or seasonal jobs to supplement your income.
- **Investments**: Generate passive income through investments in stocks, bonds, real estate, or peer-to-peer lending.
- **Side Businesses**: Start a side business based on a hobby or passion, such as selling crafts, tutoring, or writing.

Workbook Activity: Income Diversification Plan

Develop a plan to create additional income streams based on your skills and interests.

Income Source	Description	Estimated Earnings	Actions Needed
Freelancing	Offer services on a freelance basis		
Part-Time Work	Find part-time or seasonal jobs		
Investments	Generate income through investments		
Side Business	Start a business based on a hobby		

10.3.2: Managing Multiple Income Streams

Effectively managing multiple income streams ensures that you maximize your earnings and maintain financial stability.

- **Tracking Income and Expenses**: Use financial tools or apps to track income and expenses from different sources.
- **Budgeting for Variable Income**: Create a flexible budget that accounts for fluctuations in income.
- **Saving and Investing Additional Income**: Prioritize saving and investing any additional income to build wealth and enhance financial security.

Workbook Activity: Multiple Income Management Plan

Create a plan for managing and maximizing multiple income streams.

Task	Description	Frequency	Notes
Track Income and Expenses	Use financial tools to track finances	Ongoing	
Flexible Budgeting	Create a budget that accounts for variable income	Monthly	
Save and Invest	Prioritize saving and investing additional income	Ongoing	

10.3.3: Leveraging Technology for Income Diversification

Technology can help you find and manage additional income streams more efficiently.

- **Freelance Platforms**: Use platforms like Upwork, Fiverr, or Freelancer to find freelance work.
- **Online Marketplaces**: Sell products or services through online marketplaces like Etsy, eBay, or Amazon.
- **Investment Apps**: Utilize investment apps like Robinhood, Acorns, or Wealthfront to manage your investments.
- **Gig Economy Apps**: Participate in the gig economy through apps like Uber, Lyft, TaskRabbit, or Instacart.

Workbook Activity: Technology Utilization Plan

Identify and use technology platforms to diversify and manage your income streams.

Platform Name	Description	Frequency of Use	Notes
Upwork	Find freelance work	Weekly	

Etsy	Sell products online	Monthly	
Robinhood	Manage investments	Daily	
Uber	Participate in the gig economy	As needed	

10.4: Ensuring Adequate Insurance Coverage

Having the right insurance coverage is essential for protecting your financial well-being and providing a safety net in times of need.

10.4.1: Types of Insurance Coverage

Understand the different types of insurance coverage and their importance in building financial resilience.

- **Health Insurance**: Covers medical expenses and protects against high healthcare costs.
- **Life Insurance**: Provides financial support to your beneficiaries in the event of your death.
- **Disability Insurance**: Replaces a portion of your income if you become unable to work due to a disability.
- **Homeowners/Renters Insurance**: Protects your home and personal belongings against damage or loss.
- **Auto Insurance**: Covers vehicle-related expenses, including accidents, theft, and liability.

Workbook Activity: Insurance Coverage Assessment

Assess your current insurance coverage and identify any gaps that need to be addressed.

Insurance Type	Current Coverage	Recommended Coverage	Actions Needed
Health Insurance			
Life Insurance			
Disability Insurance			
Homeowners/Renters Insurance			

Auto Insurance

10.4.2: Evaluating and Updating Your Insurance Policies

Regularly reviewing and updating your insurance policies ensures that you maintain adequate coverage.

- **Reviewing Coverage Levels**: Assess your current coverage levels to ensure they meet your needs.
- **Comparing Insurance Providers**: Shop around and compare different insurance providers to find the best rates and coverage.
- **Updating Policies**: Update your policies to reflect any changes in your life circumstances, such as marriage, children, or a new home.

Workbook Activity: Insurance Policy Review Plan

Create a plan for regularly reviewing and updating your insurance policies.

Task	Description	Frequency	Notes
Review Coverage Levels	Assess current coverage to ensure adequacy	Annually	
Compare Providers	Shop around for best rates and coverage	Annually	
Update Policies	Reflect changes in life circumstances	As needed	

10.4.3: Understanding and Utilizing Insurance Benefits

Maximizing your insurance benefits helps you get the most value from your policies.

- **Understanding Policy Details**: Familiarize yourself with the details of your insurance policies, including coverage limits, deductibles, and exclusions.
- **Utilizing Preventive Services**: Take advantage of preventive services offered by your health insurance,

such as annual check-ups and screenings.

- **Filing Claims Effectively**: Know the process for filing claims and keep necessary documentation to support your claims.

Workbook Activity: Insurance Benefits Utilization Plan

Create a plan to understand and utilize your insurance benefits effectively.

Task	Description	Frequency	Notes
Review Policy Details	Familiarize with coverage limits, deductibles, and exclusions	Annually	
Utilize Preventive Services	Take advantage of health insurance preventive services	Annually	
File Claims Effectively	Know the claims process and keep documentation	As needed	

10.5: Improving Financial Literacy

Improving your financial literacy is a continuous process that enhances your ability to make informed financial decisions and build financial resilience.

10.5.1: Identifying Financial Literacy Resources

Accessing reliable financial literacy resources helps you stay informed and improve your financial knowledge.

- **Books and Articles**: Read books and articles by financial experts on topics such as investing, budgeting, and retirement planning.
- **Online Courses and Webinars**: Enroll in online courses and attend webinars to learn about personal finance and advanced financial strategies.

- **Financial News and Blogs**: Follow financial news outlets and blogs to stay updated on market trends and financial insights.

Workbook Activity: Financial Literacy Resource Plan

Identify and utilize financial literacy resources to enhance your financial knowledge.

Resource Name	Type (Book, Course, etc.)	Frequency of Use	Notes

10.5.2: Building Financial Skills

Developing key financial skills enables you to manage your finances more effectively and build resilience.

- **Budgeting and Expense Tracking**: Learn how to create and manage a budget, and track your expenses to stay on top of your finances.
- **Investing**: Gain knowledge about different investment options, risk management, and portfolio diversification.
- **Debt Management**: Understand strategies for managing and reducing debt, including debt repayment methods and credit score improvement.
- **Retirement Planning**: Learn how to plan for retirement, including setting savings goals, choosing retirement accounts, and developing a withdrawal strategy.

Workbook Activity: Financial Skills Development Plan

Create a plan to develop key financial skills and enhance your financial literacy.

Skill	Description	Learning Resources	Timeline
Budgeting	Create and manage a budget		
Investing	Learn about		

	investment options and risk managemen t		
Debt Management	Understand debt repayment methods and credit improvemen t		
Retirement Planning	Plan for retirement and develop a withdrawal strategy		

10.5.3: Seeking Financial Education and Guidance

Seeking financial education and guidance from professionals can provide valuable insights and support for building financial resilience.

- **Financial Advisors**: Work with financial advisors to receive personalized advice and strategies tailored to your financial goals.
- **Workshops and Seminars**: Attend financial workshops and seminars to gain knowledge and network with other individuals interested in personal finance.
- **Mentorship and Networking**: Seek mentorship from experienced professionals and build a network of individuals who can provide support and guidance.

Workbook Activity: Financial Education and Guidance Plan

Develop a plan to seek financial education and guidance from professionals and experienced individuals.

Resource or Person	Type (Advisor, Workshop, etc.)	Frequency of Use	Notes

Chapter Quiz

1. What are the key components of financial resilience, and why are they important?

    - Answer: Emergency savings, diversified income sources, adequate insurance coverage, and financial literacy are key components of financial resilience. They help manage financial shocks, reduce stress, and enhance financial flexibility.

2. How can you build and maintain an emergency fund?

    - Answer: Determine the size of your emergency fund based on your monthly expenses, set up a dedicated savings account, automate savings, reduce expenses, increase income, and prioritize replenishing the fund after use.

3. What are some ways to diversify your income sources?

    - Answer: Offer freelance or consulting services, find part-time or seasonal work, generate passive income through investments, and start a side business based on a hobby or passion.

4. How can you ensure adequate insurance coverage for financial resilience?

    - Answer: Review and update your insurance policies regularly, compare different providers, understand policy details, utilize preventive services, and know the claims process.

5. Why is improving financial literacy important, and how can you do it?

    - Answer: Improving financial literacy

enhances your ability to make informed financial decisions and build resilience. You can do this by accessing reliable financial literacy resources, developing key financial skills, and seeking education and guidance from professionals.

Chapter 10: Key Takeaways

1. **Build Financial Resilience**: Understand the key components of financial resilience and set goals to strengthen them.

2. **Establish and Maintain an Emergency Fund**: Calculate the size of your emergency fund, create a savings plan, and ensure it is used wisely and replenished as needed.

3. **Diversify Income Sources**: Identify additional income streams, manage multiple sources effectively, and leverage technology to find and manage opportunities.

4. **Ensure Adequate Insurance Coverage**: Review, update, and utilize your insurance policies to protect against financial risks.

5. **Improve Financial Literacy**: Access financial literacy resources, develop key financial skills, and seek education and guidance from professionals.

With a solid foundation in financial resilience and adaptability, you are well equipped to handle life's uncertainties and continue progressing toward your financial goals. In Chapter 11, we will explore the concept of financial independence and early retirement (FIRE). We will discuss the principles and strategies of the FIRE movement, including aggressive saving, investing, and lifestyle adjustments, to achieve financial independence and the freedom to retire early. By understanding and implementing these strategies, you can work towards achieving financial freedom and enjoying a fulfilling life on your terms.

CHAPTER 11: ACHIEVING FINANCIAL INDEPENDENCE AND EARLY RETIREMENT (FIRE)

T he concept of Financial Independence and Early Retirement (FIRE) has gained popularity as individuals seek to achieve financial freedom and retire early. The FIRE movement encourages aggressive saving, mindful spending and strategic investing reaching a point where you no longer need to work for money. This chapter will provide an in-depth exploration of the FIRE principles, strategies for achieving financial independence, and methods for maintaining a fulfilling early retirement. By implementing these strategies, you can work towards achieving financial freedom and enjoy a life of your choosing.

11.1: Understanding The Fire Movement

The FIRE movement is built on the idea that financial

independence allows you to retire early and live life on your own terms. This section will explore the origins, principles, and different approaches within the FIRE community.

11.1.1: Key Principles of FIRE

The FIRE movement is grounded in several key principles that guide individuals towards financial independence.

- **Aggressive Saving and Investing**: The cornerstone of FIRE is saving a significant portion of your income—typically 50% or more—and investing it wisely.
- **Frugality and Mindful Spending**: Emphasizes living below your means and making intentional spending choices that align with your values and goals.
- **Passive Income Generation**: Building streams of passive income, such as dividends, rental income, and interest, to support your lifestyle without active work.
- **Financial Independence Metrics**: Understanding and calculating key metrics such as your FI number (the amount needed to be financially independent) and safe withdrawal rate (the percentage of your portfolio you can withdraw annually without depleting it).

Workbook Activity: FIRE Goal Setting

Define personal financial independence and retirement goals, and calculate your FI number based on desired lifestyle and expenses.

Goal	Description	Actions Needed	Timeline
Financial Independence	Define what FI means to you		
Retirement Goals	Outline desired lifestyle in retirement		
FI Number Calculation	Calculate FI number based on expenses		

11.1.2: Setting Your FIRE Goals

Setting clear and achievable goals is crucial for staying

motivated on the path to FIRE.

- **Defining Financial Independence**: Clarify what financial independence means to you and how it aligns with your life goals.
- **Calculating Your FI Number**: Determine the amount of money you need to be financially independent by calculating your annual expenses and applying a safe withdrawal rate (typically 4%).
- **Determining Your Desired Lifestyle**: Consider how you want to spend your time in early retirement, including hobbies, travel, and activities.

Workbook Activity: FIRE Lifestyle Planning

Plan your desired lifestyle in early retirement, including activities, hobbies, and travel.

Aspect of Lifestyle	Description	Estimated Cost	Notes
Housing	Type and location of residence		
Travel	Frequency and type of travel		
Hobbies and Activities	Desired hobbies and activities		
Health and Wellness	Fitness, healthcare, and well-being		

11.2: Building A High Savings Rate

A high savings rate is essential for achieving financial independence. This section will provide strategies for reducing expenses and increasing income to maximize your savings.

11.2.1: Reducing Expenses

Reducing expenses without compromising your quality of life is a key aspect of the FIRE philosophy.

- **Identifying and Cutting Unnecessary Expenses**: Analyze your spending habits and identify areas where you can cut back without sacrificing essentials.

- **Practicing Frugality**: Embrace a frugal lifestyle by focusing on value, avoiding waste, and making intentional spending choices.

- **Using Budgeting Tools**: Utilize budgeting tools and apps to track your spending and ensure you stay within your budget.

Workbook Activity: Expense Reduction Plan

Identify discretionary expenses to cut and create a monthly budget focused on maximizing savings.

Expense Category	Current Monthly Spending	Target Monthly Spending	Actions Needed
Housing			
Transportation			
Food			
Entertainment			
Subscriptions			

11.2.2: Increasing Income

Boosting your income accelerates your journey to financial independence. This subsection will explore various strategies for increasing your income.

- **Freelancing and Side Hustles**: Offer your skills and services on a freelance basis or start a side hustle that generates additional income.

- **Leveraging Skills and Talents**: Use your existing skills and talents to find higher-paying opportunities or take on additional responsibilities at work.

- **Investing in Education and Training**: Invest in further education and training to increase your earning potential and qualify for higher-paying roles.

Workbook Activity: Income Boosting Plan

List potential income sources and estimated earnings, and develop a plan to implement additional income streams.

Income Source	Description	Estimated Monthly Earnings	Actions Needed

Freelancing	Offer services on a freelance basis		
Side Hustles	Start a side business or gig		
Additional Job	Take on part-time or additional work		
Skill Development	Invest in education and training		

11.3: Investing For Financial Independence

Investing is a critical component of the FIRE strategy. This section will cover investment vehicles, building a diversified portfolio, and strategies for long-term growth.

11.3.1: Choosing Investment Vehicles

Selecting the right investment vehicles is essential for building a robust and resilient portfolio.

- **Stocks and Bonds**: Understand the role of stocks and bonds in your portfolio, balancing growth potential and stability.
- **Real Estate**: Consider real estate investments, including rental properties and REITs, for diversification and passive income.
- **Tax-Advantaged Accounts**: Maximize contributions to tax-advantaged accounts such as 401(k)s, IRAs, Roth IRAs, and HSAs.
- **Index Funds and ETFs**: Utilize low-cost index funds and ETFs to gain broad market exposure and minimize fees.

Workbook Activity: Investment Strategy Plan

Define investment goals and risk tolerance, and choose appropriate investment vehicles for your FIRE strategy.

Investment Vehicle	Description	Target Allocation (%)	Actions Needed

Stocks	Individual stocks or mutual funds		
Bonds	Government or corporate bonds		
Real Estate	Rental properties, REITs		
Tax-Advantaged Accounts	401(k), IRA, Roth IRA, HSA		
Index Funds and ETFs	Broad market index funds, ETFs		

11.3.2: Building a Diversified Portfolio

Diversification is key to managing risk and achieving steady returns. This subsection will provide strategies for building and maintaining a diversified portfolio.

- **Asset Allocation**: Determine the appropriate mix of asset classes based on your risk tolerance and investment goals.
- **Rebalancing Your Portfolio**: Regularly review and adjust your portfolio to maintain your target asset allocation.
- **Managing Risk**: Implement strategies to manage risk, such as diversification, dollar-cost averaging, and avoiding market timing.

Workbook Activity: Portfolio Diversification Plan

Create a diversified investment portfolio based on risk tolerance and goals, and set a schedule for regular portfolio rebalancing.

Asset Class	Target Allocation (%)	Current Allocation (%)	Actions Needed
Stocks			
Bonds			
Real Estate			

Alternative Investments			

11.4: Managing Lifestyle And Spending In Early Retirement

Managing your lifestyle and spending in early retirement is crucial for ensuring your financial independence lasts. This section will explore strategies for mindful spending and generating passive income.

11.4.1: Mindful Spending in Retirement

Practicing mindful spending helps you prioritize your expenses and avoid lifestyle inflation.

- **Prioritizing Spending**: Focus on spending money on what truly matters to you and brings you joy.
- **Avoiding Lifestyle Inflation**: Resist the temptation to increase your spending as your income grows.
- **Using Budget Tracking Tools**: Continue using budgeting tools to monitor your spending and stay within your budget.

Workbook Activity: Retirement Spending Plan

Create a retirement budget focused on mindful spending and list prioritized expenses and discretionary spending limits.

Expense Category	Estimated Monthly Spending	Notes
Housing		
Utilities		
Food		
Healthcare		
Travel		
Hobbies and Entertainment		

11.4.2: Generating Passive Income in Retirement

Generating passive income is vital for sustaining your lifestyle in early retirement without depleting your savings.

- **Sources of Passive Income**: Explore sources such as dividends, rental income, royalties, and interest.
- **Managing Passive Income Streams**: Regularly review and manage your passive income streams to ensure they continue to meet your needs.
- **Growing Passive Income**: Reinvest a portion of your passive income to grow your wealth and enhance financial security.

Workbook Activity: Passive Income Plan

Identify and develop passive income sources, and create a plan to manage and grow passive income in retirement.

Passive Income Source	Description	Estimated Monthly Income	Actions Needed
Dividends	Income from stocks and mutual funds		
Rental Income	Income from rental properties		
Royalties	Income from intellectual property		
Interest	Income from savings and bonds		

11.5: Overcoming Challenges On The Fire Journey

The path to financial independence and early retirement is not without challenges. This section will explore common obstacles and strategies for overcoming them.

11.5.1: Dealing with Market Volatility

Market volatility is inevitable, and managing it effectively is crucial for maintaining your investment strategy.

- **Understanding Market Cycles**: Recognize that market fluctuations are normal and part of the investment process.

- **Staying Invested During Downturns**: Avoid panic selling and maintain a long-term perspective.
- **Diversification and Risk Management**: Use diversification and risk management techniques to mitigate the impact of market volatility.

Workbook Activity: Market Volatility Management Plan

Develop a plan for managing market volatility and maintaining your investment strategy.

Strategy	Description	Actions Needed	Timeline
Understand Market Cycles	Learn about market fluctuations		
Stay Invested	Avoid panic selling		
Diversify Investments	Maintain a diversified portfolio		

11.5.2: Maintaining Motivation and Discipline

Staying motivated and disciplined is essential for achieving long-term goals.

- **Staying Focused on Goals**: Regularly review your goals and progress to stay motivated.
- **Celebrating Milestones**: Celebrate small achievements along the way to maintain enthusiasm.
- **Building a Support Network**: Connect with others in the FIRE community for support, advice, and motivation.

Workbook Activity: Motivation and Discipline Plan

Identify strategies for maintaining motivation and discipline on your FIRE journey.

Strategy	Description	Actions Needed	Timeline
Regularly Review Goals	Assess progress and stay focused		
Celebrate Milestones	Acknowledge and celebrate achievements		
Build Support Network	Connect with the FIRE community		

Chapter Quiz

1. What are the key principles of the FIRE movement, and how do they contribute to financial independence?

    - Answer: The key principles include aggressive saving and investing, frugality and mindful spending, passive income generation, and understanding financial independence metrics. These principles help build a robust financial foundation and create multiple income streams to support early retirement.

2. How can you achieve a high savings rate to accelerate your journey to FIRE?

    - Answer: By reducing unnecessary expenses, practicing frugality, using budgeting tools, increasing income through freelancing, side hustles, or additional jobs, and investing in education and training to boost earning potential.

3. What investment strategies are essential for achieving financial independence?

    - Answer: Choosing the right investment vehicles (stocks, bonds, real estate, tax-advantaged accounts, index funds, and ETFs), building a diversified portfolio, and regularly rebalancing your portfolio to manage risk and achieve steady returns.

4. How can you manage lifestyle and spending in early retirement to ensure financial independence lasts?

    - Answer: Practice mindful spending by prioritizing expenses that bring joy, avoid lifestyle inflation, use budgeting tools, and generate passive income through dividends, rental income, royalties, and interest.

5. What are some strategies for overcoming challenges on the path to FIRE?

- Answer: Deal with market volatility by understanding market cycles, staying invested during downturns, and using diversification and risk management techniques. Maintain motivation and discipline by regularly reviewing goals, celebrating milestones, and building a support network within the FIRE community.

Chapter 11: Key Takeaways

1. **Understand the FIRE Movement**: Familiarize yourself with the principles of FIRE, including aggressive saving, frugality, passive income, and financial independence metrics.

2. **Set Clear FIRE Goals**: Define what financial independence means to you, calculate your FI number, and plan your desired lifestyle in early retirement.

3. **Achieve a High Savings Rate**: Reduce unnecessary expenses, practice frugality, use budgeting tools, and increase income through various means.

4. **Invest Wisely**: Choose appropriate investment vehicles, build a diversified portfolio, and regularly rebalance your investments.

5. **Manage Lifestyle and Spending in Retirement**: Practice mindful spending, avoid lifestyle inflation, and generate passive income to sustain your lifestyle.

6. **Overcome Challenges**: Manage market volatility, stay motivated and disciplined, and connect with the FIRE community for support.

CONCLUSION

Recap Of Key Concepts

As we conclude "Rebuilding Financial Stability: A Practical Guide to Debt-Free Living and Future Planning," let us recap the key concepts and strategies covered in this book. Our journey began with understanding your current financial situation, setting achievable goals, and building a strong financial foundation. We explored practical steps for managing debt, improving credit, saving, and budgeting. With a solid foundation in place, we delved into investing, risk management, and estate planning to secure your financial future. Finally, we embraced the principles of the FIRE movement, advanced financial strategies, and ongoing financial planning to sustain financial independence and enjoy early retirement.

Emphasizing The Importance Of Financial Literacy

Financial literacy is the cornerstone of financial independence and stability. Throughout this book, we have highlighted the importance of continuous learning and staying informed about financial trends and strategies. By enhancing your financial knowledge, you can make informed decisions, adapt to changes, and navigate financial challenges with confidence.

The Role Of Discipline And Consistency

Achieving and maintaining financial stability requires discipline and consistency. The strategies and principles outlined in this book emphasize the need for regular financial reviews, mindful spending, and disciplined saving and investing. Consistently applying these practices will help you stay on track and achieve your financial goals.

Adapting To Life Changes And Challenges

Life is full of unexpected events and changes that can affect your financial situation. This book has provided you with the tools and strategies to adapt to these changes and manage financial risks effectively. By building financial resilience and staying flexible in your planning, you can navigate life's challenges while maintaining financial stability.

Finding Purpose And Fulfillment In Financial Independence

Financial independence is not just about money; it is about having the freedom to live life on your own terms. As you achieve financial independence, it is important to find purpose and fulfillment beyond financial goals. Pursue your passions, engage in meaningful activities, and build a life that brings you joy and satisfaction.

Encouraging A Holistic Approach To Financial Planning

A holistic approach to financial planning considers all aspects of your life, including your personal values, goals, and relationships. This book has encouraged you to integrate your financial plan with your overall life plan, ensuring that your financial decisions align with your broader aspirations and well-being.

Inspiring Future Generations

By embracing the principles and strategies outlined in this book, you can inspire future generations to achieve financial independence and stability. Share your knowledge and experiences with family and friends, and encourage them to take control of their financial futures. Together, we can build a financially literate and empowered society.

Final Thoughts

"Rebuilding Financial Stability: A Practical Guide to Debt-Free Living and Future Planning" has equipped you with the knowledge and tools to achieve financial independence and build a secure future. Remember that the journey to financial stability is ongoing, and staying committed to your financial goals is key to long-term success. Embrace the principles of financial literacy, discipline, and adaptability, and you will be well on your way to a prosperous and fulfilling life.

Thank you for joining us on this journey. We wish you all the best in your financial endeavors and hope that this book serves as a valuable resource as you continue to build and sustain your financial independence.

APPENDIXES

APPENDIX A: FINANCIAL TOOLS AND TEMPLATES

This appendix provides practical financial tools and templates to help you implement the strategies discussed throughout the book. Use these resources to create a personalized financial plan, track your progress, and make informed financial decisions.

A.1: Monthly Budget Template

Monthly Budget Template

Income Source	Estimated Amount	Actual Amount
Salary/Wages		
Freelance/Side Hustles		
Investments		
Other Income		
Total Income		

Expense Category	Estimated Amount	Actual Amount
Housing		
Utilities		
Food		
Transportation		
Insurance		
Debt Repayment		
Savings		

Investments		
Entertainment		
Subscriptions		
Miscellaneous		
Total Expenses		

Category	Amount
Net Income	

A.2: Debt Repayment Plan

Debt Repayment Plan

Debt	Total Amount Owed	Interest Rate (%)	Minimum Payment	Additional Payment	New Balance
Loan 1					
Loan 2					
Credit Card 1					
Credit Card 2					
Total Debt					

Month	Total Payment	Principal Paid	Interest Paid	Remaining Balance
January				
February				
March				
...				
December				

A.3: Savings Goal Tracker

Savings Goal Tracker

Savings Goal	Target Amount	Monthly Contribution	Total Saved	Target Date
Emergency Fund				
Vacation Fund				
Down Payment Fund				
Education Fund				
Retirement Fund				
Total Savings				

A.4: Investment Portfolio Tracker

Investment Portfolio Tracker

Asset Class	Investment Type	Initial Investment	Current Value	Annual Return (%)
Stocks				
Bonds				
Real Estate				
Mutual Funds				
ETFs				
Cash/Cash Equivalents				
Total Portfolio				

A.5: Retirement Planning Worksheet

Retirement Planning Worksheet

Retirement Goal	Description	Target Amount	Monthly Contribution	Total Saved	Target Date
Desired Retirement Age					
Estimated Monthly Expenses in Retirement					
Social Security Income					
Pension Income					
Other Income Sources					
Total Retirement Savings					

A.6: Net Worth Statement

Net Worth Statement

Assets	Value
Cash and Cash Equivalents	
Savings Accounts	
Checking Accounts	
Investments	
Retirement Accounts	
Real Estate	
Personal Property	
Other Assets	
Total Assets	

Liabilities	Amount Owed
Mortgage	
Auto Loans	
Student Loans	
Credit Card Debt	
Other Liabilities	
Total Liabilities	

| Net Worth | |

A.7: Financial Goal Setting Worksheet

Financial Goal Setting Worksheet

Goal	Description	Target Amount	Monthly Contribution	Total Saved	Target Date
Short-Term Goals					
Medium-Term Goals					
Long-Term Goals					

Use these templates to organize your financial information, set clear goals, and track your progress over time. By regularly updating these documents, you can stay focused on your financial objectives and make informed decisions to achieve financial stability and independence.

APPENDIX B: ADDITIONAL RESOURCES

This appendix provides a collection of additional resources to further assist you in your financial journey. These resources include books, websites, tools, and organizations that can offer valuable information and support.

B.1: Recommended Books

Personal Finance and Budgeting

- "The Total Money Makeover" by Dave Ramsey
- "Your Money or Your Life" by Vicki Robin and Joe Dominguez
- "The Simple Path to Wealth" by JL Collins
- "Rich Dad Poor Dad" by Robert T. Kiyosaki
- "The Millionaire Next Door" by Thomas J. Stanley and William D. Danko

Investing

- "The Intelligent Investor" by Benjamin Graham
- "A Random Walk Down Wall Street" by Burton G. Malkiel
- "Common Stocks and Uncommon Profits" by Philip Fisher
- "One Up On Wall Street" by Peter Lynch
- "The Little Book of Common Sense Investing" by John

C. Bogle

Financial Independence and Retirement Planning

- "Early Retirement Extreme" by Jacob Lund Fisker
- "Work Optional: Retire Early the Non-Penny-Pinching Way" by Tanja Hester
- "How to Retire Happy, Wild, and Free" by Ernie J. Zelinski
- "The Bogleheads' Guide to Retirement Planning" by Taylor Larimore, Mel Lindauer, Richard A. Ferri, and Laura F. Dogu
- "The 4-Hour Workweek" by Timothy Ferriss

B.2: Helpful Websites

Personal Finance

- https://www.nerdwallet.com/
- https://www.mint.com/
- https://www.thebalance.com/
- https://www.investopedia.com/

Investing

- https://www.morningstar.com/
- https://seekingalpha.com/
- https://www.marketwatch.com/
- https://finance.yahoo.com/

Financial Independence and Retirement

- https://www.mrmoneymustache.com/
- https://www.choosefi.com/
- https://www.madfientist.com/
- https://firehub.eu/

B.3: Online Tools and Calculators

Budgeting and Expense Tracking

- https://www.youneedabudget.com/

- https://www.mint.com/
- https://www.everydollar.com/
- https://www.pocketguard.com/

Investment Calculators

- Vanguard Retirement Nest Egg Calculator
- Schwab Retirement Savings Calculator
- Bankrate Investment Calculator

Debt Repayment Calculators

- Debt Snowball Calculator by Undebt.it
- Credit Karma Debt Repayment Calculator

B.4: Financial Education Courses

Online Courses

- Coursera Personal Finance Courses
- edX Personal Finance Courses
- Khan Academy Personal Finance
- Udemy Personal Finance Courses

B.5: Supportive Organizations

Consumer Financial Protection Bureau (CFPB)

- https://www.consumerfinance.gov/
- Provides resources and tools to help consumers make informed financial decisions.

National Foundation for Credit Counseling (NFCC)

- https://www.nfcc.org/
- Offers financial counseling and education to help consumers manage their debt and improve their financial well-being.

Financial Planning Association (FPA)

- https://www.financialplanningassociation.org/
- Provides resources and support for financial planning professionals and individuals seeking financial

planning advice.

Better Business Bureau (BBB)

- https://www.bbb.org/
- Helps consumers find trustworthy businesses and charities, and offers resources on financial and consumer issues.

AARP (American Association of Retired Persons)

- https://www.aarp.org/
- Provides resources and advocacy for individuals over 50, including financial planning and retirement advice.

Use these additional resources to deepen your financial knowledge, find support, and access tools that can assist you on your journey to financial stability and independence. By leveraging these resources, you can stay informed, make better financial decisions, and achieve your financial goals.

APPENDIX C: GLOSSARY OF FINANCIAL TERMS

This appendix provides definitions for key financial terms used throughout the book. Understanding these terms will help you better grasp the concepts and strategies discussed.

A

Asset Allocation

The process of distributing investments among different asset classes, such as stocks, bonds, and real estate, to balance risk and return.

Assets

Anything of value owned by an individual or organization, including cash, investments, property, and personal belongings.

B

Bonds

Debt securities issued by corporations, municipalities, or governments to raise capital, typically offering fixed interest payments over a specified period.

Budget

A financial plan that outlines expected income and expenses over a specific period, helping individuals manage their money and achieve financial goals.

C

Capital Gains

The profit realized from the sale of an asset, such as stocks or real estate, when the selling price exceeds the purchase price.

Credit Score

A numerical representation of an individual's creditworthiness, based on their credit history, used by lenders to assess the risk of lending money.

D

Debt-to-Income Ratio

A financial metric that compares an individual's monthly debt payments to their monthly gross income, used by lenders to assess borrowing capacity.

Diversification

An investment strategy that involves spreading investments across various asset classes and sectors to reduce risk.

E

Emergency Fund

A savings account set aside for unexpected expenses or financial emergencies, typically covering three to six months' worth of living expenses.

Equity

The ownership interest in an asset or company, calculated as the difference between the asset's value and any outstanding debt.

F

FIRE (Financial Independence, Retire Early)

A movement focused on achieving financial independence and retiring early through aggressive saving, investing, and frugal living.

Fixed Expenses

Regular, recurring expenses that remain relatively constant over time, such as rent, mortgage payments, and insurance premiums.

G

Gross Income

The total income earned before any deductions, such as taxes and retirement contributions.

I

Index Fund

A type of mutual fund or exchange-traded fund (ETF) designed to replicate the performance of a specific market index, such as the S&P 500.

Inflation

The rate at which the general level of prices for goods and services rises, reducing purchasing power over time.

L

Liabilities

Financial obligations or debts owed by an individual or organization, including loans, credit card balances, and mortgages.

Liquidity

The ease with which an asset can be converted into cash without significantly affecting its value.

M

Mutual Fund

An investment vehicle that pools money from multiple investors to invest in a diversified portfolio of stocks, bonds, or other securities.

N

Net Worth

The value of an individual's assets minus their liabilities, representing their overall financial position.

P

Passive Income

Earnings generated with minimal effort, such as rental income, dividends, and royalties.

Portfolio

A collection of investments held by an individual or organization, including stocks, bonds, real estate, and other assets.

R

Risk Tolerance

An individual's ability and willingness to endure fluctuations in the value of their investments.

Roth IRA

A type of individual retirement account that allows for tax-free withdrawals in retirement, funded with after-tax contributions.

S

Stocks

Securities representing ownership in a company, entitling the shareholder to a portion of the company's profits and assets.

Savings Rate

The percentage of income saved and invested, an essential factor in achieving financial independence and early retirement.

T

Tax-Advantaged Account

An investment account that offers tax benefits, such as a 401(k),

IRA, or HSA, designed to encourage saving for retirement or healthcare expenses.

Tax-Loss Harvesting

An investment strategy that involves selling securities at a loss to offset capital gains and reduce taxable income.

W

Withdrawal Rate

The percentage of an investment portfolio withdrawn annually during retirement, with the goal of ensuring the portfolio lasts throughout the retiree's lifetime.

Use this glossary as a reference to familiarize yourself with essential financial terms and concepts. By understanding these terms, you will be better equipped to navigate your financial journey and make informed decisions.

APPENDIX D: FREQUENTLY ASKED QUESTIONS (FAQS)

This appendix addresses common questions and concerns about financial planning, debt management, investing, and achieving financial independence. Use these FAQs as a quick reference to clarify concepts and guide your financial decisions.

D.1: Financial Planning

Q: What is the first step in creating a financial plan?

A: The first step is to assess your current financial situation. This includes calculating your net worth, understanding your income and expenses, and identifying your financial goals.

Q: How often should I review my financial plan?

A: It's recommended to review your financial plan at least annually, or more frequently if there are significant changes in your financial situation or goals.

D.2: Debt Management

Q: What is the best way to tackle high-interest debt?

A: Prioritize paying off high-interest debt first, using strategies such as the debt avalanche method (paying off debt with the highest interest rate first) or the debt snowball method (paying off the smallest debts first to build momentum).

Q: Should I consolidate my debt?

A: Debt consolidation can be beneficial if it simplifies your payments and reduces your interest rates. However, it's important to ensure that the consolidation terms are favorable and that it doesn't lead to additional debt.

D.3: Saving and Budgeting

Q: How much should I have in my emergency fund?

A: Aim to save three to six months' worth of living expenses in your emergency fund. This amount can vary based on your individual circumstances, such as job stability and family size.

Q: What percentage of my income should I save each month?

A: A common recommendation is to save at least 20% of your income each month. However, this can vary based on your financial goals and obligations.

D.4: Investing

Q: How do I start investing with little money?

A: Start by investing small amounts in low-cost index funds or ETFs. Many online brokers offer accounts with no minimum balance requirements, allowing you to begin investing with as little as $50 or $100.

Q: What is diversification, and why is it important?

A: Diversification involves spreading your investments across different asset classes (such as stocks, bonds, and real estate) to reduce risk. It helps protect your portfolio from significant losses if one investment performs poorly.

D.5: Retirement Planning

Q: How much do I need to save for retirement?

A: The amount needed for retirement depends on your desired lifestyle, expected expenses, and retirement age. A common rule of thumb is to aim for 25 times your annual expenses saved by the time you retire.

Q: What is the 4% rule?

A: The 4% rule is a guideline for retirement spending,

suggesting that you can withdraw 4% of your retirement savings each year without significantly depleting your portfolio over a 30-year period.

D.6: Financial Independence and Early Retirement (FIRE)

Q: What is the FIRE movement?

A: The FIRE (Financial Independence, Retire Early) movement encourages aggressive saving, mindful spending, and strategic investing to achieve financial independence and retire early.

Q: How can I achieve a high savings rate?

A: Increase your savings rate by reducing expenses, practicing frugality, and boosting your income through side hustles, freelancing, or career advancements.

D.7: Risk Management and Insurance

Q: What types of insurance do I need?

A: Essential types of insurance include health insurance, life insurance, disability insurance, homeowners or renters insurance, and auto insurance. The specific types and amounts of coverage will depend on your individual circumstances.

Q: How often should I review my insurance policies?

A: Review your insurance policies annually or whenever you experience a major life event, such as marriage, the birth of a child, or purchasing a home.

D.8: Estate Planning

Q: What is the purpose of estate planning?

A: Estate planning ensures that your assets are distributed according to your wishes after your death, minimizes estate taxes, and provides for your loved ones.

Q: What documents are essential for estate planning?

A: Key estate planning documents include a will, a durable power of attorney, a healthcare proxy, and, in some cases, trusts.

D.9: Taxes

Q: How can I minimize my tax liability?

A: Strategies to minimize tax liability include contributing to tax-advantaged accounts (such as 401(k)s and IRAs), taking advantage of tax credits and deductions, and employing tax-loss harvesting in your investment portfolio.

Q: Should I hire a tax professional?

A: Hiring a tax professional can be beneficial if you have a complex financial situation, own a business, or want to ensure you are taking full advantage of available tax strategies.

Use these FAQs as a quick reference to address common financial questions and guide your decision-making process. By understanding these concepts, you can navigate your financial journey with greater confidence and clarity.

ABOUT THE AUTHOR

Robert Knight

Robert Knight is a seasoned financial expert with over 15 years of experience in personal finance and wealth management. Having helped countless individuals and families achieve financial stability, Robert combines practical advice with a deep understanding of the financial landscape. His expertise spans across budgeting, debt management, investment strategies, and retirement planning. Robert is dedicated to empowering readers with the knowledge and tools they need to take control of their finances and build a secure future. In addition to writing, Robert enjoys hiking and exploring the great outdoors and is passionate about financial education and literacy.

www.ingramcontent.com/pod-product-compliance
Lightning Source LLC
Chambersburg PA
CBHW071920210526
45479CB00002B/496